J Hughes

Welsh Reformers

Biographical Sketches of Eminent Welshmen, Foremost in Promoting...

J Hughes

Welsh Reformers

Biographical Sketches of Eminent Welshmen, Foremost in Promoting...

ISBN/EAN: 9783337008741

Printed in Europe, USA, Canada, Australia, Japan

Cover: Foto ©ninafisch / pixelio.de

More available books at **www.hansebooks.com**

BIOGRAPHICAL SKETCHES OF EMINENT WELSHMEN,

FOREMOST IN PROMOTING THE CAUSE OF RELIGION IN WALES DURING THE TUDOR AND STUART DYNASTIES;

CONTAINING ALSO

A MEMOIR OF ROWLANDS, LLANGEITHO,

INCLUDING HIS SERMONS.

BY THE
REV. J. HUGHES,
INCUMBENT OF GWERNAFIELD, MOLD, NORTH WALES.

"Reformation work is God's work, and good works the fruit."—HENRY.

LONDON:
JAMES NISBET & CO., 21 BERNERS STREET.
MDCCCLXVII.

PREFACE.

THE original object of this publication was simply to furnish a new English edition of Rowlands' sermons; but at the suggestion of various friends, it was deemed advisable to condense the sermons, without sacrificing any matter which they contained, and prefix a brief outline of Rowlands' life, with a few others who had distinguished themselves in all religious movements which materially concerned the welfare of their country, the interest of religion, and the salvation of souls.

Tillotson, in his lifetime, was regarded as the greatest preacher either amongst the living or the dead, but posterity has not endorsed, but rather reversed, that decision. Whereas Rowlands was the greatest preacher Wales had ever known, whether long since resting from their labours, or now occupying their pulpits. Yet from his sermons it would be quite as impossible to arrive at such conclusion as it would be to transform to paper the fire and unction which characterized his preaching.

The fire of Calvin, the eloquence of Massillon, and the piety of Fenelon, seemed all concentrated in Rowlands' character.

It is a source of deep regret that our limits would only admit of an indirect allusion to many eminent and conscientious men amongst both Churchmen and Non-conformists: amongst whom history assigns the foremost rank to such men as Lloyd, Bishop of St Asaph,* who was one of the seven bishops imprisoned in the Tower, Walter Cradock, William Erbury, Richard Davies the Quaker, and James Owen, a learned dissenter, Stephen Hughes, and Samuel Jones, both ejected ministers, the former an inti-

* The life of this worthy prelate is delineated by Macaulay in a style as singular for its beauty as it is unshaken in the testimony he bears to the Bishop's unimpeachable character. It is gratifying to learn that the descendants of this Christian hero still live among us,—Charles Spencer Lloyd, Esq., Leaton Knolls, Shrewsbury, ranks first in his claims of lineal descent from this venerable stock. A life-like portrait of Bishop Lloyd was to be seen at the National Gallery about three years ago.

mate friend of the venerable Vicar of Llandovery, the latter a profound divine and accurate scholar; John Penry,* more commonly known as Martin-Marprelate; Thomas Llewellyn, who so ably aided the Society for Promoting Christian Knowledge to print many thousand additional Bibles; the self-denying Hugh Owen; and the famous Daniel Williams, the noble founder of the Red Cross Street Institution in London.

The itinerant character of the Non-comformists generally gives their ministers a world-known celebrity. The stationary character of a parish clergyman is less known, but his work is not less solid. And however much they may differ in opinions on minor points, it is hoped, that both the stationary clergyman and the itinerant minister will find some day that they have been fighting for the same truths, building up the same faith, and trusting in, and resting on, the merits of the same blessed Saviour, Jesus Christ our Lord.

* Disraeli in his "Calamities and Quarrels of Authors," relates some incidents in Penry's history, which are not generally known.

CONTENTS.

	PAGE
The Reformation,	1
William Salesbury,	14
Bishop Davies,	25
Bishop Morgan,	36
Edmund Prys,	50
Bishop Parry,	58
Bishop Griffith,	64
John Davies, D.D.,	74
Rhys Prichard,	83
Griffith Jones,	80
Rowlands' Memoir,	108
Sermon I.,	143
Sermon II.,	157
Sermon III.,	176
Sermon IV.,	180
Sermon V.,	201
Sermon VI.,	215
Sermon VII.,	228
Sermon VIII.,	241
Subscribers' Names,	253

THE REFORMATION.

MUCH misunderstanding generally prevails respecting the Reformation effected in the Church in the sixteenth century. The Romanists condemn the Reformation as a great schism, which, they say, is also a great sin. During centuries previous to this event, they regarded the constitution of the Church of England, in matters of doctrine and of discipline, as being one with the Church of Rome, the latter, as a matter of course, being invested with the supremacy. It is generally admitted, that the constitution of the two Churches remained in unison with each other as long as the doctrine and discipline of Rome remained pure and apostolical; yet this conformity, as long as it prevailed, was at all times an encroachment and an usurpation. When errors and corruptions crept into the Church of Rome, the same errors and corruptions were *forced* upon the

Church of England. Both Churches had gone astray. At the Reformation the Church of England returned to primitive doctrine and practice. The Church of Rome, loving darkness rather than light, remained in her delusions. Therefore the Church of England did not secede from the Church of Rome, but the Church of Rome seceded from the truth.

The truth of our observation is tested by the evidence of history. We therefore appeal to the history of the Church of CHRIST from its first establishment in this country.

It is generally supposed that Christianity was first preached in Britain by one of the apostles. It is certain that the Christian religion flourished here at a very early period, which the history of the Christian Church amply testifies.[1]

The signatures of three British bishops[2] appended to the canons enacted at the Council of Arles, held about A.D. 314, furnish a strong presumptive evidence that the Christian Church had been established in Britain some considerable time before that period. This primitive Christian Church, adorned with meekness, sim-

---

[1] Stillingfleet, Origines Britannicæ. Blunt's History of the Reformation.

[2] Eborius, Bishop of York; Restitutus, Bishop of London; and Adelfius, Bishop de civitate Colonia Londinenson,—supposed to be Colchester.

plicity, and truth, was apostolic in its origin, pure in doctrine and discipline, and in every respect independent of the Church of Rome.

Another proof of its early existence is amply furnished in the history of the martyr, S. Alban, who suffered death during the Diocletian persecution, A.D. 303, when the British Church, in common with the rest of Christendom, experienced the dire calamity of that fatal scourge.[1]

When the Roman Empire was threatened by the fierce incursions of the Goths, the Emperor Honorius withdrew the Roman troops, and released the Britons from Roman sway. This occurred in 410. But no sooner were the Roman soldiers withdrawn, than the Pagan Saxons, aware of the defenceless condition of the country, made a descent upon Britain. The Church they pillaged, her monuments they destroyed, her archives they ransacked, and her records they burnt. The Arian and Pelagian heresies were again elements which disturbed her peace, corrupted her doctrine, and threatened her very existence. Yet she survived all these onslaughts, and at a time when she could not longer conceal her weakness, she firmly maintained her independence. For when Augustine

[1] See an interesting little volume of this subject, by Rev. R. Wilson Evans.—Tales of the Early British Church.

was sent into Britain, A.D. 1567, by Pope Gregory the Great, there were still found British bishops who refused submission to the papal emissary. And although it is willingly admitted, that to Gregory[1] and Augustine—whose designs towards this country were actuated by the highest motives and the best Christian spirit—the Church of England owed its vitality and restoration, yet the *independency* of the British Church was in no manner affected by this timely succour. The interference of Rome at this time must be looked upon as the friendly succour of a more flourishing sister towards a sister in distress;—not as the authoritative assistance of a mother towards her daughter, owing existence to her at the first, and bound to pay her due submission and obedience for the future.

It would not be amiss here to state, that in Great Britain there were two distinct Churches, acting independently of each other,—the British

---

[1] The doctrines of the Church of Rome were at this time unpolluted. Gregory himself declared " that whoever desired to be styled universal bishop was antichrist, and further averred that none of his predecessors had consented to be so styled. Augustine, also, though an emissary of Rome, had been ordained bishop by Etherius, Archbishop of Arleate (now Arles), in Gaul. Therefore he received his ordination from Gallic, not Roman hands.—See Bishop Godwin, de Conversione Britannicæ.

and the Anglican Church, both branches of the universal Church, and both acting independently of Rome. "The Britons had churches of their own, built after a fashion of their own: they had their own saints: their own hierarchy:—The British bishops, attending a council as such, held no intercourse with the Angles even in Bede's time, but looked on them as Samaritans. Moreover, the jealousy wherewith the Welsh long afterwards regarded all ecclesiastical interference on the part of England, their resolute assertion of their right to a Metropolitan of their own at St David's, and their actual exercise of that right till the time of Henry I., argues the same difference in the rock from which the English and British Churches were originally hewn."[1]

But independent of the British Church, we maintain, that from the mission of S. Augustine until the invasion of the Danes, and the reign of King Alfred, the Church of England continued, as she had been from the beginning, a branch of the true Catholic or universal Church. She, in common with many other European Churches, was, doubtless under trials of persecutions and corruptions, much indebted to the Church of Rome for counsel, learning, and guidance. Yet she produced divines and his-

---

[1] Blunt on the Reformation.—p. 3.

torians of her own; was governed for the most part by her own native bishops, and framed her own regulations in matters of discipline,—matters indifferent in themselves, but not essentially necessary.[1]

The bishops of Rome, it is true, attempted to exercise dominion over her, and were more or less successful, at different times, and in different places; but their supremacy was continually protested against, and was evidently not a right, but an usurpation and encroachment, which different kings at different times successfully resisted, and which Henry VIII. flung finally away.

During a long period of friendly intercourse between the Church of England and the Church of Rome, it had not been unusual for the Primate of England to receive, as a compliment, his pall from Rome. By degrees, and in process of time, this custom gave occasion to the Church of Rome to assume an authority, implying primacy as well as supremacy, and indicating not only that the bishops of Rome possessed power and jurisdiction over the clergy and realm of England, but that the Pope's sanction to the appointment of the English Metropolitan was

[1] Things indifferent pertain to discipline, rather than doctrine. Baptism is essential, the mode of administration is non-essential.

absolutely necessary. This assumed authority England always resisted, and *never* acknowledged. As early as the year A.D. 798, the British bishops, with their clergy, addressed a letter to Pope Leo III., protesting against the necessity of their Metropolitan receiving his pall from Rome, because Church records furnished them with ample evidence that some of their archbishops had not received it at all.

Blunt, in his History on the Reformation, adduces ample evidence to the same effect from Bede,—the honest Anglo-Saxon ecclesiastical historian. "It is curious," saith he, "to observe, that within two hundred years after the foundation of the Anglo-Saxon Church, Aldfrid, a king of Northumbria, feels himself called upon to resist the interference of the Pope in a case of appeal, and actually refuses to listen to his recommendation."[1]

Pope Alexander furthered William the Conqueror's designs in invading England. Yet, as soon as the Conqueror found his throne firmly established, he not only resisted all interference on the part of Rome, but would not allow his subjects to recognize any one as Pope, of whom he had not himself first approved; nor to admit ecclesiastical canons not first ratified by his own

---

[1] Blunt on the Reformation.

authority; nor to obey any papal bull without his royal sanction. The Pope intended William as an instrument to inspire the Anglo-Saxon with the same sacred feeling toward himself, wherewith his Holiness was regarded in his own country, admitting that the "Anglo-Saxon conducted their ecclesiastical government with an acknowledgment of primacy in the See of Rome, but without much idea of its title to dominion and authority."[1] Yet this very authority the king himself refused to recognize, alleging the independency of the Church of England, and repudiating the encroachments of the Church of Rome.

The concessions made by King John, when excommunicated by Pope Innocent III., consenting to pay tribute to Rome (known as Peter's pence), were repudiated by Edward III., and when Pope Urban V. threatened to cite him to the Court of Rome for his refusal and insubordination, the king immediately (A.D. 1367), laid the matter before his Parliament. That assembly unanimously declared that King John could not, without the consent of the nation, subject his kingdom to such foreign taxation, and expressed their determination to support their king under circumstances of such illegal pretensions.

[1] Hume,—Vol. I., p. 107.

Grostête, the Bishop of Lincoln in the reign of King Henry III., protested against papal aggression, refused to obey any papal bulls, and actually denounced the Pope as a heretic and an antichrist.

Again, in the reign of King Edward III., Wycliffe, with a large number of laity and clergy, raised his voice against Romish usurpations and corruptions. He might well be styled the forerunner of the Reformation, whose name will be known as long as truth will be loved.

In order to produce another testimony, in a form more tangible and reliable, we refer to the statutes of this realm, and no statute of any kind amongst the annals of its history formally recognizes the power of the Pope in this country. His pretensions are ignored by all constitutional authority, and his claims are not recognized by a single act of Parliament.

William I. and II., in a manner characteristic of themselves, sternly forbade their subjects to recognize any act emanating from Rome, which had not their sanction and approbation.

Henry I. firmly resisted the gigantic schemes which Pope Gregory VII. had planned for his own aggrandisement; but Stephen and John —the one an usurper, the other a coward and a tyrant—with timidity unbecoming royalty, submitted to be swayed by Popes. Their minds were haunted by phantoms, and their hearts sank at the sound of excommunication. Yet, notwithstanding the temporary ascendancy of the Pope's supremacy, a statute was enacted in the twentieth year of Henry III., in which it is set forth, that all the canons and decrees of the Church of Rome had hitherto been of no force in England. In the same reign was also enacted another statute, declaring it *penal* to procure any presentations to benefices in England from the Court of Rome, and any person carrying an appeal to the Court of Rome would be regarded as an outlaw. These enactments during the reigns of Richard II., Henry IV., V., and VI., were probably never very rigidly enforced: but still their existence amongst the statutes of the realm of England was bitterly galling to the assumed supremacy of Rome. And Pope Martin V., in a letter written to Henry VI., threatens, with no milder punishment than eternal *damnation*, any one who should dare obey them. Notwithstanding these papal fulminations, the statutes were confirmed from time to time, but probably incompletely executed: for during the reigns of Edward IV., Richard II., and Henry VII., the Pope assumed a supremacy and jurisdiction which were foreign to the constitution of this country, and condemned by the highest authority in the land.

Having thus briefly glanced at the history of the Church, from its first origin and establishment in Great Britain, until the time of the Reformation, the summary of our evidence leads us to the conclusion, that the supremacy of Rome was only an assumed power, unknown to the constitution, and never recognized by one single act of Parliament. Separation, therefore, could be no schism, and the rejection of Romish errors could be no sin, of the British Church. At the time of the Reformation, the Church, like the prodigal son, only returned, as it were, to her own home,—her ancient doctrine and discipline practised in her early days. Had the Church not then effected her escape, the thraldom of tyranny would be still her lot, and the Council of Trent would have fastened its seal to errors which had their origin in heathen rites, whose idolatrous teaching is a disgrace to religion, profanes God's holy temple, and tramples upon the prerogatives of the Most High.

For centuries things were ripening towards this great event, when, in the dispensation of Providence, the Church of England should finally shake off the yoke of Rome. Amongst the Benedictines there was no peace. The seculars eyed the regulars with envy, jealousy, and hostility, that burned deep in their bosom. When these were wrangling amongst themselves, a new order, assuming the badge of poverty, appeared in the Church. These were the Franciscans. They were divided into four divisions,—the Franciscans, Dominicans, the Carmelites, and the Augustines. No sooner, however, than the four orders became distinct bodies, the camp of poverty was a scene of confusion, and the badges of penury had become the butt of ridicule. Amongst themselves there were jealousy, hatred, and malice, so that, in the time of Erasmus and Luther, their rivalry was an object of ridicule, and their whole system was as rottenness to the bones of the Romish Church.

All these, and many more circumstances, made the Reformation inevitable; so that when Henry VIII. wanted the support of his subjects against the interference of the Pope, his subjects wanted the king's support against papal supremacy. If the fire burnt with unusual rapidity, it was because all the trees were dry. The Church had been consumed, but not destroyed. After being purified from error, and relieved from foreign usurpation, from her ashes she sprang again into life, and in all original beauty she resumed her apostolic form. The Church having endured many vicissitudes, struggling with poverty, persecution, and ignorance, yet having no sooner emerged from obscurity and insignificance, than she again plunged into grievous errors. In every stage she was the same Church, though under various circumstances, but at the Reformation she became free and pure as at first. And if her temporalities were now taken away, she would be still the same Church, and must still so remain, with her bishops, priests, and sacraments, for what no earthly power originally gave, no earthly power can ever take away.

To restore the Church to primitive doctrine and practice, the Welsh Reformers materially effected, when they furnished her with the oracles of divine truth, in a language known as the ancient British tongue.[1]

---

[1] The reader wishing to ascertain further facts relating to acts affecting the Church, is referred to Statute of Merton, 20 H. III., cap. 9; Statute 9 E. II., Artic. Cleri. 16; Stat. 25 E. III.; 11 H. IV., cap. 37; 3 H. V., cap. 4; 1 H. VII., f. 10.

WILLIAM SALESBURY.

William Salesbury,—a name as renowned for his patriotism in Wales, as ever William Tell was known to be in Switzerland. Time and distance separated the two patriots from each other. Yet kindred feelings burned in their bosoms and animated their hearts,—a love for their country and their countrymen. Tell displayed his feelings by his bow and arrow, and wrought deliverance for his country. Salesbury manifested his love and zeal with his pen and paper, and chased the gloom of ignorance and superstition by the light of knowledge and truth. The mountain-tops of his picturesque country, capped with clouds of mist and darkness, were, in Salesbury's eyes, only true emblems of the superstition and ignorance which sat brooding over his countrymen's hearts, to remove which, he devoted the best energies of his mind, and ran the risk of his life. The name of Salesbury occupies a prominent position in the history of our country. When Bolinbroke took the king a prisoner at Flint Castle, at first his demeanour was respectful, but he soon changed his tone, and commanded the king's horses to be brought forth, when two wretched nags made their appearance. The king was set on the one, and the Earl of Salisbury on the other. Again, we find that the stewardship of Chester, with Hawarden, was granted to William Montacute, Earl of Salisbury." It continued in his family till the death of his great nephew, John, Earl of Salisbury."[1] It is highly probable that William Salesbury sprang from the honourable branches that had grown upon this ancient and venerable stock. For about a century later, several families of distinction, bearing respectively *the name of Salisbury and Salesbury*, resided in different parts of the country; yet most of them traced their pedigree to Thomas Salesbury, of Lleweni, near Denbigh, who was generally acknowledged as the head of the clan, though himself not improbably a descendant of Thomas, Earl of Salisbury, who, in the reign of Henry V., petitioned Parliament for the recovery of estates forfeited to the king after his father's attainder. When Abelard, the illustrious mediæval philosopher and divine, was de-

[1] Pennant's Tour in Wales.—pp. 48, 49.

livering his lectures in Paris, it is said in his biography, that John of Salisbury was one of his most devoted hearers. Salesbury is a name that stands eminent for literary abilities.

Whether, then, the Celtic or Teutonic element constituted William Salesbury's character, is of little consequence, and admits of no easy solution. For in several Welsh MSS.[1] he is sometimes called William Salbri, sometimes William Salsbri, but never William Salesbury. What he inherited from his father's side is doubtful. What he inherited from his mother's side is certain. Foulk Salesbury, William's father, married Gwenhwyfar, the only daughter and heiress of Rhys Ab Einion Vychau Plasisaf Llanrwst. Soon after the noble race of Tudor had ascended the throne of Great Britain, William Salesbury was born at Llanrwst. Of his early career little is known. He did not frequent the banks of the Conway for its fish, nor the hill-sides of his country for the chase. His habits were retired and contemplative. His manners were gentle and inobtrusive; yet, withal, he was very firm. Nothing would easily shake his resolutions, and his energy in pursuit of knowledge knew no fatigue. Literature was his pleasure, and languages his delight.

---

[1] Preface to Edeyrn dafod aur, by Ab Ithel.

With what honours his academical course was distinguished at Oxford, or with what avidity he afterwards digested the law at Lincoln's Inn, remains amongst the remnants of tradition, and cannot now be stated as facts. But that he was a great linguist cannot be denied. Henry Parry,—a descendant from a very respectable family in Flintshire, a very learned philologist, and called by Dr Davies, in his Preface to his Welsh Dictionary, " Vir linguarum cognitione insiquis,"—informs us, that Salesbury was thoroughly acquainted with nine different languages besides English and Welsh, viz., Chaldee, Syriac, Hebrew, Arabic, Greek, Latin, French, Italian, and Spanish. His patriotism, however, is not established upon the extent of his linguistic attainments, but rather from being the author of the first Welsh book ever printed in the Welsh tongue. This was a singular production, and from the variety of its contents, doubtless a very useful book, whose peculiar adaptation for all times and seasons savours of a mixture which humours the imagination, whilst it feeds the mind. It was a species of an almanac, which not merely referred to the days, weeks, and months of the year, but it also contained an elaborate treatise upon the great characteristics of the Welsh tongue. We are, however, not left to grope in darkness touching our spiritual concerns, for it also contained the Creed, the Lord's Prayer, the Ten Commandments, the seven virtues of the Church, and lastly—and perhaps not the least important feature at the time—directions respecting the "usual games" which were much indulged in at a later period, as a sort of Sunday exercise.

The variety of subjects it embraced naturally needed this extraordinary volume to appear in a quarto form. It was printed in 1546. This publication was soon followed by another:—" A Dictionary in Englyshe and Welshe, moche necessary to all such Welshmen as will speedly learn the Englyshe tongue, thought unto the Kynges Majestie very mete to be sette for the use of his Graces subjects in Wales; whereunto is prefixed a little Treatyse of the Englyshe pronunciation of the letters."

Again, in 1550, he published another book:— "An Introduction to the Pronunciation of the Letters in the British Tongue,"—a second edition of which appeared (revised and improved) seventeen years after the first appearance of its prototype. Lord Macaulay somewhere observes, that the English language in Shakespeare's time had acquired that elasticity, power, and mould, that it was inferior to none, the Greek alone excepted. Probably he knew nothing of the exhaustless resources and the rich diction of the

Welsh language, which is loathe to yield precedence to the Greek itself. Which is the eldest sister is difficult to determine. That they are twin sisters, cognate tongues, can be easily perceived. That the old British tongue, even in our day, reckons about four thousand words more than can be found in any English dictionary, is a fact which cannot be gainsaid. The language is rich, copious, and musical; it gives a soul to the objects of Sense, a spirit to Poetry, and a body to the abstractions of Philosophy. It was a mine of wealth to a mind like that of Salesbury's, wherein he loved to dig for its treasures, that his countrymen might enjoy the fruit of his labours. But all his works fall into insignificance compared with his self-denying exertions in translating the New Testament into Welsh. It was enacted in 1563, that the Bible should be used in every church in Wales, in the Welsh tongue, by March 1566. The work of translating the sacred volume was entrusted to the Bishops of St David's, Llandaff, Bangor, St Asaph, and Hereford, who, under a penalty, were enjoined to see the work properly executed by the specified time,—they, fully aware of Salesbury's zeal for the Protestant religion, his philological attainments, and great abilities, unanimously fixed upon him as the best qualified person to undertake so important a charge.

The result was, that Salesbury's Welsh black-lettered New Testament, so highly prized, and now so rare, was issued from the press in 1567, and although three hundred years have well nigh since elapsed, the translation, nevertheless, has scarcely undergone any change, and the passages which have since been corrected are not now supposed to be inferior to the original, nor a less perfect transcript of the Greek version.[1] To accomplish so great a work in so short a time, required intense application, much diligence, and great learning, and the only assistance he seems to have received was from the Bishop of St David's, and Thomas Huet, precentor of the same cathedral; the latter translated *the Book of Revelation*, which bears his initials, T. H. C. M.;[2] the bishop, the first Epistle to Timothy, the Epistle to the Hebrews, the General Epistle of St James, and the two Epistles of St Peter. Sir John Wynn of Gwydir—a gentleman of eminent abilities, whose writings remained in MSS. for upwards of two hundred years, a contemporary of Salesbury, and his survivor of more than thirty years,—informs us, that Salesbury was engaged on a translation of the Old Testament, and resided for two years with the Bishop of St David's

---

[1] *Vide* Gwladgarwr on Salesbury's Translation.
[2] Cantor Meneviæ.

for that object, during which time "he was very far onward, and had gone through with it if variance had not happened between them for the general sense and etymology of one word, which the bishop would have one way, and William Salesbury another, to the great loss of the old British and mother tongue; for being together, they drew homilies, books, and divers other tracts in the British tongue, and had done far more if that unlucky division had not happened; for the bishop lived five or six years after, and William Salesbury about twenty-four, but gave over writing, more was the pity, for he was a rare scholar, and especially an Hebrecian, whereof there was not many in those days." We would fain demur to the statement alleged by Sir John, that Salesbury ceased writing after his rupture with the bishop, for he had now succeeded to his father's estates—his elder brother Robert dying without male issue—which enabled him to take up his residence at the mansion of Plasisaf; yet it is a well known fact, that during a great portion of this time he lived at a place called Caedû, near the summit of a narrow inaccessible glen on the river Aled, in the parish of Llansannan, about seven miles distant from Llanrwst. This he built as a place of concealment, neccessary during the Marian persecution, from his well known attachment to the truth and his zeal for the Protestant religion. In this secluded retreat Salesbury constructed a private chamber, where his writing materials were securely excluded from any intrusion. An entrance to this private chamber could not be gained either by a flight of stairs, or by the more ordinary means of a ladder, commonly used at that time, and which, to this day, amongst the numerous modern improvements, has not been wholly dispensed with on the mountains of Wales, but by climbing inside the chimney, from which a private door led to his private chamber. As late as the year 1857, traces of this bulky chimney, which at one time had emitted clouds of smoke and excluded all suspicion, could be distinctly seen amongst the ruins of Caedû. In many mountainous districts of Wales, coals are unknown as fuel. Peat is used instead. It is burnt on the hearth in large quantities, and gives the kitchen an air of domestic comfort in a manner which our parlours often fail to furnish. But wherever the custom prevails, the dimensions of the chimneys are constructed on a spacious scale, always in proportion to the amount of peat consumed on the hearth, and the quantity of smoke emitted through the aperture.

On such a cheerful hearth stood Salesbury's little table, on which were placed his books, paper, and pen, but when the barking of his dog outside created the least suspicion of strangers, our aged patriot, *plus* pen and paper, vanished through the smoke up the chimney, and felt the same security in his little asylum in the roof of his house, as the early Christians had experienced in the caves of the rock. It is not impossible but that at this time he translated the Epistles and Gospels used on Sundays and festivals in the Church throughout the year, and that this was the last work which engaged his attention ere he was summoned to relinquish his labour in order to receive his reward. The date of his departare hence remains amongst the uncertainties of time. History, which records the labours of his useful life, did not chronicle the day of his death. Length of days had crowned his hoary head. He lived during the greatest part of the Tudor dynasty, and witnessed the reign of five sovereigns. No monument at this day marks the place of his burial. Yet greater monuments still exist, which testify of him, that, though being dead, he yet speaketh. The genius which excited Salesbury to honourable pursuits and patriotic deeds, is not extinct in his descendants, and the branches[1] which now

[1] E. R. G. Salesbury, Esq., late M.P. for Chester, whose only surviving son is the sole male representative of the two most honourable names recorded in Welsh biography; his

flourish, reflect honour and renown upon the source whence they have sprung. In closing our remarks upon the life of this great and good man, we pay him that tribute wherewith genius honours wisdom, and award him that honour wherewith virtue regards sanctity. As long as the Bible will be read in the Welsh tongue, the name of William Salesbury will be revered by the Welsh nation. As a patriot his countrymen were dear to his heart, but as a Christian the truth was dear to his soul. The one he loved with the affection of a brother, the other he embraced with the simplicity and sincerity of a child.

Note.—We purposely omitted many other works which emanated from Salesbury's pen, viz., his "Battery against the Pope's High Altar," his "Exemplar of Rhetoric," also certain Prayers, with directions, &c., as space would not admit of any remarks.

father claims William Salesbury as his great ancestor, whilst his mother traces her lineal descent to Bishop Morgan.

BISHOP DAVIES

RICHARD DAVIES, generally known by the name of Bishop Davies, was the son of Davydd ab Gronw, curate of Gyffin, who resided at a place called Plas-y-person, near Conway, Carnarvonshire. After Davies had been elevated to the espiscopal bench, and translated from St Asaph to St David's, his successor at St Asaph bore the same cognomen, so there were two contemporary Welsh bishops bearing, respectively, the name of Davies. But the illustrious bishop of St David's so far outshone his brother of St Asaph, as to have eclipsed the fame of the latter. These two prelates were born and bred in the same neighbourhood, and if they were not brought up together at the same school, they travelled together at the same time to the same college, and were at length raised to occupy the same prominent and dignified position in the Church. The same year as Thomas Davies was elevated to the see of St Asaph, Richard

Davies was translated to the bishopric of St David's. Yet at the present day there is only one generally known as Bishop Davies, and that distinction we voluntarily yield to the Bishop of St David's. Davies of St Asaph was revered for his piety, gentleness, and charity. His quiet and retired life, by reason of its even and regular course, glided gently along the ordinary channel, without attracting any general attention, or creating any peculiar sensation. Not so Bishop Davies of St David's. He was like a great meteor, a comet, or a flood, whose course excites our fear and our admiration, but which leaves on the mind an impression of greatness, and power, and strength. Bishop Davies' early education was conducted under his father's roof, and superintended by his father's care. Whether he quitted this homely seminary for a more public school before he left his father's house for his university career, must now remain amongst the remnants of tradition, and what laurels he won at New Inn, Oxford, must also share the same fate. Little indeed is known of his history before 1550. Before he was nearly fifty years of age, King Edward VI. presented him to the Vicarage of Burnham, which he held with the rectory of Maidsmoreton, Buckinghamshire. The mournful event which witnessed the early close of Edward's short reign, created through the heart of England feelings of dismal apprehensions, which were only too soon realized. Mary's Romish predilections were too well known, and her marriage with Philip of Spain coupled her name and her religious creed with all the horrors of the Inquisition. Davies' feelings for the Reformed faith he did not feign to conceal. When Gardiner and Bonner cried out for the stake and the faggot, it is said that the Queen was of their mind, in opposition even to the papal legate, who recommended toleration. Under these circumstances, Davies was not only deprived of his preferments, but had to flee his country in order to save his life. Englishmen, by scores, flocked to Geneva, and amongst these exiles was Davies with his family.

They had only just made their escape in time, for no sooner had they reached Geneva than the bloody persecution had begun in England. Bonner, whose brutal and savage nature would not be satiated with anything less than his brethren's blood, executed the Queen's commands with all haste and savage pleasure. He had a keen relish to see those with whom

[1] Amongst the many then exiled at Geneva was John Bodley, a descendant of an opulent Devonshire family, and father of the famous Sir Thomas Bodley, the noble founder of the Bodleian Library.

he had once kneeled before the same altar, tortured to death by means of racks and fire. Such odious barbarity, practised indiscriminately, seized the whole country with horror and alarm. Most of these Englishmen who had retired to Geneva were persons of substance and wealth, upon whose charity, it is said, that Davies for some time found means of subsistence. But his independency of feelings, joined with a proper sense of honour, would not allow him, whilst capable of any action, to be a burden even to friends. His was not a proud mind, but a magnanimous spirit. He applied himself with indomitable perseverance to master the French tongue. The rapidity with which he overcame all difficulties evinces his great mental abitities, for in a short time he was not only able to understand that language, but to speak it correctly and fluently. He now obtained a cure, in which he preached during the remainder of his exile, which enabled him to support his wife and family without being a burden to others. During his exile were born to him three sons, Thomas, Peregrine, and Jerson. The Marian persecution, however, soon ceased in England, when he immediately returned to take possession of his churches, which he held *in commendam* with the bishopric of St Asaph, to which see he was elevated in 1560. And the next year he was translated to the bishopric of St David's.

At present it is usual to confer the degrees of doctor in divinity before a bishop is consecrated, whereas it appears that in Bishop Davies' time the dignity did not always precede, but often followed episcopal elevation, and in this instance the dignity of the degrees was conferred six years subsequent to the dignity attached to his episcopal order. As a scholar he had long merited that distinction which such honours bestow. However distinguished other scholars might be in the general branches of literature, few were found more eminent than Bishop Davies. His learning and proficiency were not unknown to Queen Elizabeth, when Her Majesty should pass by so many English prelates, and come to Wales for a gentleman who could translate a few books of the Old Testament from the original Hebrew. His great efforts in this respect had spread his fame far and wide, for he was, doubtless, the first who suggested, and the first that ever attempted, the translation of the Bible into his own native tongue. With this view he invited the co-operation of the most skilful linguists of the age, whom he, with his usual hospitality, sumptuously entertained at his own palace. At the head of this learned conclave stood pre-eminently the renowned patriot and ripe scholar, William Salesbury. The bishop who had once, in the hour of adversity, succumbed to live upon the charity of friends, now, in the hour of prosperity, acknowledged his gratitude with bounteous and unbounded liberality. His establishment at Abergwili was conducted on a princely style. The scale accorded with his own taste and character, whose mind displayed magnanimity in every action of his life.

Sons of noblemen were proud to shelter under his roof, and the best families in the country deemed it an honour to see their children's education conducted under the patronage of so distinguished a prelate.

We may here relate a little incident wherein the bishop is presented in another light than strictly in his episcopal character, yet wherein he displayed all that magnanimity of action so characteristic of his life. Sir John Parrot, who, acting as a friend to the Earl of Leicester—a very extensive landed proprietor in that county—attempted to claim some property in favour of the earl, which by right belonged to the bishop. A consciousness of right inspires even the weak and timid with courage and strength, but it invested the bishop with the strength of a giant and the authority of a prince. The prelate confronted the baronet, and in few words, more telling than blows, Sir John was awed, and glad to beat retreat, lest the bishop, wielding both temporal and spiritual power, should execute his threat, and inflict on the baronet, as a mark of his displeasure, such sore punishment as would not merely follow his departure out of the country, but his departure out of the world. This is by no means unnatural, for the superstition of the age, fostered by a blind priesthood, had exercised a fearful sway over men's minds, and the country had not yet experienced its emancipation from such baleful influence, which the light of truth can only remove, and which the Bishop of St David's was ever making such noble efforts to disseminate throughout the principality of his native country.

Syr John Wynne of Gwydir would lead us to infer, that in points of linguistic discriminations, when it came to tests and balances, which required great nicety of skill to give a doubtful sentence its true bearing, a doubtful expression its exact meaning, and a doubtful word its true etymology, Bishop Davies was not equal to William Salesbury. The bishop had pure gold, as well as the skill to beat that gold into such a thin leaf that it appeared to cover massive bullions. His great mind only scanned great things, and, like itself, only admired great objects. He was not an inapt type of the description the great Robert Hall furnished of his father's character:—" He appeared to the greatest advantage upon subjects where the faculties of most men fail them, for the natural element of his mind was greatness." Principles and systems he vastly loved, but rules and details he greatly disliked. He could look with unbounded admiration *through the telescope* at the sun, the moon, and the stars, but it was fatiguing to him to examine the leaf, the blade, and the insect even, through the microscope. He could write sermons equal to Tillotson, but he could not examine evidence like Paley. Like Atterbury he *would* be first and foremost in every contest, and, at all hazards, win laurels for the day; but he lacked the discriminating powers of Bently, who could ransack old dusty volumes, collate old manuscripts, and raise a monument to his fame, which excited the admiration of posterity.

William Salesbury, who was a great genius, also took great pains. He would not disdain to explore old pits where remained any grains of gold, nor would he cease digging until he brought up the gold in his hand. Bishop Davies, on the other hand, could not sacrifice time to search for trifles—he must have bullions, or none. The two giants, who had hitherto lived on terms of great friendship, now confronted each other on a question of etymology. The bishop *would* not yield, Salesbury *could* not concede. Friendship, which before flourished like a palm tree, ceased to exist when the *roots* were unsettled. The layman retired to his solitude, and lived for many years; the bishop remained at his palace, but died within six years.

Independent of the bishop's translations of many books of the New Testament, he also translated the Liturgy of the Church of England; but he is best remembered, and mostly admired by his excellent epistle dedicated to "all the Welsh, especially those within his own diocese, desiring a renewal of the ancient Catholic Faith by the light of the Gospel of CHRIST." This breathes the very spirit of the early Christian Church, and fully acknowledges that the ancient catholic faith had been guided by some other light than that of the Gospel of Christ. The renewal of this ancient catholic faith by the light of gospel truth, is the very essence of that reformation which was effected in the sixteenth century, whose fruit we now reap, and whose blessings may we long enjoy.

Our attention, however reluctant, must not leave unnoticed some unfavourable impressions whereby Bishop Davies has been unsparingly censured; and it is a matter of deep regret that so distinguished a prelate should, in the management of his diocese, have left room for the breath of complaint to heave its sighs. Yet when the subject is closely examined, and duly weighed, *pro and con.*, the enormity of the injustice rapidly diminishes, if it does not wholly disappear. It is asserted by his successor, that in order to provide for his numerous family " all his lands, even to his doors, were in lease by his predecessor," &c. It must not be forgotten that even bishops are only men, and the truth that it is " human to err," no one doubts. We must not, therefore, be blind to the fact, that the assertion is made by a *successor*, who, probably from an interested point of view, might be, with a distorted sight, looking through his own glasses. Censures should be less sparing when the law is not violated; and the act of leasing Church property was no contravention of law, nor an extraordinary act to a man who, in all difficulties, soared above difficulties, yet no stranger to the bitter morsel which the hands of charity could have scarcely made palatable. Those who stigmatize this good man's name with being worldly, would probably, with the same breath, if he had not provided for his family, call him something worse than an infidel.

Some pieces of his poetry are still extant, but as a poet he is not known,—distinction in this branch of literature he was never destined to attain. His acknowledged abilities as a Hebrew scholar of the first order were duly valued, and highly honoured when he was appointed by Queen Elizabeth to revise and compare with the original Hebrew the Books of Joshua, Ruth, and the first and second Books of Samuel, at the time Her Majesty had ordered a new translation of the English Bible, commonly known as Parker's Bible. The aged bishop, who had now seen many years, and had experienced many vicissitudes, who had done much in his day, and worked hard for his country, is at length called from his vineyard to receive his reward. He was buried at Abergwili, 1581, aged eighty years, as ripe, we hope, for glory as he was for the grave. He had struggled with many difficulties, and witnessed many trials. He manfully coped with poverty, and did honour to his affluence. When his clergy, from various parts of his extensive diocese, attended his funeral to pay him their last tribute of respect, they all felt that a *great* man had fallen in Israel.

BISHOP MORGAN.

William Morgan, D.D., Bishop of St Asaph, was a man of superior origin, and of highly revered fame. Whilst his deep learning excites our admiration, his great piety commands our deep reverence. Of his personal appearance, whether tall or short, whether of a large or slender frame, we are left to conjecture. His biographers seemed to have unconsciously slid over this, to dwell upon features more endurable and attractive,—the sterling qualities of his mind, which embodied in their action a sentiment which afterwards assumed her more familiar shape in words, "it is the mind that makes the man." And the monuments which Bishop Morgan left behind him proved the truth of the maxim in imperishable deeds.

William Morgan was born at Gwibernant, in the parish of Penmachno, Carnarvonshire. It is by no means singular that a spot so highly favoured by nature as that through which the river Conway winds its way from its source to the sea, should have given birth to the greatest geniuses of that age. William Salesbury, Richard Davies, Bishop of St David's, Thomas Davies, Bishop of St Asaph, William Morgan, the subject of our memoir, and afterwards Bishop of St Asaph, and the great antiquary and historian Sir John Wynne of Gwydir, were all, as youths, familiar with the banks of the Conway and its lovely vale. One great man observes, that there is no place in the world more picturesque and beautiful than North Wales within the small compass it occupies. We would fain say that no spot within that compass is more lovely and beautiful than the vale of Conway. The verdure of its foliage is enriched by contrast with the bareness of its mountain tops, and its loveliness assumes the appearance of nature's most delicate touches, when compared with the wildness and the ruggedness of its steep-side rocks. Among such scenery was William Morgan bred and born. He did not commence his career with Salesbury and Bishop Davies. He was probably about twenty years younger than either, yet he marked their footprints, and walked in their footsteps, and the light which they shed did not eclipse the brilliancy wherewith he shone.

Morgan is a name of true Celtic origin, renowned for its antiquity, and not unknown for its heterodoxy; but the good bishop of the sixteenth century inherited nothing but the name of the heretic of the fifth. Morgan endeavoured to repair the breaches which the Pelagian heresy of nine centuries before had made on the bulwarks of our faith. Morgan's mother's name was Lowry—a name which ranked amongst the titled of that period, but which seems almost extinct in the present age. She was the daughter of William ab John ab Madog ab Evan Tegin, of Bettws. These numerous "abs" denote a person of some distinction; and Gwibernant, the place of William Morgan's birth, was his father's own freehold property. How this paternal heritage passed into the hands of the Mostyn's, and thence to its present owner, is not easy to solve, but not difficult to conjecture. It is said that Bishop Morgan incurred great personal responsibility in restoring the chancel of his own cathedral, and in order to discharge all his debts, he sold all his property.

Of his early days and education we know little. Tradition would fain make us record as facts many things which history would scarcely warrant us to presume. We avoid the domain of tradition; but we embrace the truth, and love to investigate facts. Morgan seems as if he had been born the genius of religion. He was a man of noble and impressive mein. His countenance indicated an intellect of no mean order, and impressed all around him with feelings of reverence and love,—love sanctified by reverence, and reverence intensified by love. He practised no austerity, and assumed no gloomy countenance. He personified religion in her natural garb of unsurpassed loveliness and beauty. Its life was seen in the blade. The early stages of manhood tested its vigour, but it was a full blade. Its fruit was visible in old age; and in the time of harvest, when it was cut down, it was ripe for glory. "The righteous shall flourish like the palm tree; he shall grow like a cedar in Lebanon. Those that be planted in the house of the Lord shall flourish in the courts of our God. They shall bring forth fruit in old age."

Such were the feelings wherewith Morgan was regarded amongst his contemporary undergraduates at St John's College, Cambridge. How long he remained at that place, and with what honours his course was distinguished, are subjects which now elude our search.

The next steps which we can trace with any certainty lead us to Welshpool, in Montgomeryshire, where William Morgan had been installed as the vicar of the parish. To this living he was instituted in 1657. As a parish priest at this place, he has not left behind any record of his industry, but of his literary diligence we possess abundant evidence. What now occupied his attention was the translation of the Pentateuch into Welsh, not from the Latin Vulgate, as its contemporary into English by Miles Coverdale, nor from any Greek edition, but from the original Hebrew text. However, he only remained three years as the vicar of Welshpool before he was promoted to the Vicarage of Llanrhaiadr-yn-Mochnant,[1] where he not only completed the work he had undertaken at Welshpool, but also the translation of all the books of the Old Testament. This he had been induced to undertake by Archbishop Whitgift, with whom he had sought an inter-

---

[1] It is probable that about this time Bishop Morgan became acquainted with the eminent antiquary and learned divine, the Rev. David Powel, D.D., Vicar of Ruabon, and who was said by his contemporaries to be " in omni literarum genere maxime versatus." Dr Powel was chaplain to Sir Henry Sidney, Lord President of the Marches of Wales, who had in his possession Caradawg History of Wales, whose translation the eminent Humphry Lloyd[1] had only half completed when he could no longer work. This translation, at Sir Sidney's request, Dr Powel finished. He was also the author of many other works.—See Williams' Life of Eminent Welshmen.

[1] For the life of this eminent antiquary and scholar, see Perry's Cambrian Plutarch, Pennant's Tours in Wales.

view, owing to some dispute with his parishioners which required the archbishop's interference. Whitgift conceived a high opinion of Morgan's abilities, and urged him in the prosecution of his labours, pointing out the importance of the work, and the blessing thereby conferred on his country. Whitgift, who opposed the spread of Puritanism with all his zeal, vehemence, and learning, nevertheless encouraged the translation of the Bible into Welsh, and appointed Morgan his chaplain as a mark of his approbation and esteem for the good work he was prosecuting with such diligence and success. In 1587, Morgan had completed the translation of the whole of the Bible, and proceeded therewith to London, where he remained for more than a whole year superintending and correcting his edition as it issued forth from the press. During the whole time of his sojourn in the metropolis, he was hospitably entertained by Dean Goodman, of whose kindness and generosity he speaks with unbounded gratitude in the dedication prefixed to the work. Gabriel Goodman, Dean of Canterbury, is perhaps better known to Welshmen generally as the founder of the Grammar School at Ruthin, of which place the dean was a native. His father's name was Edward. He married Sisely, daughter of Edward Thelwall, Plas-y-ward, and carried on the trade of a silk-mercer at Ruthin. He lived about the time when surnames were generally assumed; and characteristic of his general reputation, he was honourably nick-named Goodman. As Abigail had said of her husband, "As his name is, so is he," in a different sense Edward's countrymen had endorsed the same sentiment, as his name was, so was he—Good-man.

His ancestors traced their pedigree by the usual conjunctive Ab, viz., Edward ab Thomas, ab Edward, ab Sieneyn Goch Llandyrnog, in the vale of Clwyd. But from this time Edward assumed the surname of Goodman, a name which will reflect honour upon Wales as long as Ruthin will be known among its mountains. This Edward Goodman's son, Gabriel Goodman, at that time Dean of Canterbury, an office of high dignity, forgot not his country's claims, and by his means and liberality materially aided in promoting the translation of God's Word into his countrymen's tongue; and the first copy of the entire Bible that was ever published in the Welsh tongue, was printed solely at Dean Goodman's expense.

Morgan had become a very distinguished man, and promotions, now showered down upon him, did not extinguish his light, or tarnish his reputation. He was presented now to the rectory of Llanfyllin, as well as to the sinecure rectory of Pennant Melangell. To these preferments was soon added the sinecure rectory of Denbigh. These were still but inconsiderable, and inadequate when contrasted with his eminent zeal and vast learning, which had been for many years diligently applied for the purpose of supplying a want which the Christian Church in the principality had yearned to possess for upwards of fifteen centuries.

Some of St Paul's most distinguished fellow-prisoners at Rome were amongst the most honourable members of the British nation. In the land of their captivity they first learnt man's eternal destiny, and within their prison walls they first imbibed the principles of true liberty,—the glorious liberty which is known only to the children of God. As soon as their captivity ceased, they turned their faces homeward, and planted the banner of the Cross upon British soil. It flourished for centuries, but its history lies buried under the ruins of Bangor is-y-coed monastery, which was burnt to the ground by Saxon invaders. This monastery was originally founded by Lucius, son of Coel, who was not only the first Christian king of Great Britain, but the first Christian king known in Christendon. At the time the Saxons invaded the country, Speed states that this monastery contained not fewer than 2400 monks, 1200 of whom were then massacred. Nennius, the great historian of the first five centuries of the Christian era, was one of the abbots at Bangor is-y-coed.

The dark ages, with their horrible gloom, soon began to spread over the land the images of desolation and death; yet, in the meantime, the lamp of divine light was not wholly extinguished, but lay smouldering under the dust of ages, exhibiting symptoms of life from time to time, which burst into a flame occasionally, as we learn from the life of Sion Cent,[1] whose name is so interwoven with the history of the Lollards. Still it seemed destined in the providence of God, that Bishop Morgan should have been the first honoured instrument in bringing the ark of divine covenant, whole and entire, into Wales,— no longer veiled with any mystic symbols, but known and read of all men in the known tongue of his own countrymen.

The year after Morgan had been promoted to the sinecure rectory of Denbigh, he was, by the express command of Queen Elizabeth, elevated to the Bishopric of Llandaff. At this time the infectious virulence of party spirit swept through the land like an epidemic; it assumed some-

---

[1] Sir John of Ghent.

thing of the austere character of the early Christians, but divested of the great essentials which characterized their lives and governed their actions, viz., love, charity, and peace. Bishop Morgan, who was not infected with the enthusiasm of a party, was nevertheless tried by the maxims of that austere time, and was not found wanting.

He had scarcely been six years exercising episcopal government and spiritual authority over the see of Landaff when he was translated to the diocese of St Asaph. The removal could not have been otherwise than very gratifying in more senses than one, for his predilections for North Wales were natural and strong; yet he was not destined to meet with that gratification which earthly hopes too often nourish. For the see of Landaff, which mourned his removal in 1601, saw the see of St Asaph, which had been blessed with such a good prelate, grieve over his grave in 1604.

Yorke's "Royal Tribes of Wales" furnishes a remarkable correspondence between this good bishop and the eminent antiquary, Sir John Wynne of Gwydir. Sir John claimed the merit of the bishop's promotions, owing to the influence which he had exercised in his behalf. The good bishop, not denying the allegation, but qualifying his obligations, stating that Sir

John estimated the favours he conferred far beyond their value, or the benefits accrued therefrom. His benefactor, presuming upon his kind offices, wanted to obtain a lease of the rectory of Llanwrst. This, which was too much the custom of that age, met from Bishop Morgan a direct and positive refusal, alleging that his conscience would not allow him to sanction an act which he considered dishonest and sacrilegious. His reply is couched in such strong terms as indicate a mind of unshaken resolution, fortified by a conscience which frowned upon favours that interfered with his charge as an overseer of God's Church. "Your request," saith the bishop, "is such, that in granting it I should prove myself an unhonest, unconscionable, and irreligious man.—You, a sacrilegious robber of my church, a perfidious spoiler of my diocese, and an unnatural hinderer of preachers and good scholars, the consideration of which would be a continual terror and torment to my conscience." Sir John, in his "Biographical Memoirs," speaks of Bishop Morgan as a superior scholar, well versed in Greek and Hebrew, and alludes to his good works in restoring the chancel of his cathedral, but betrays some feelings of irreconciliation which had been doubtless occasioned by the bishop's stern refusal. This feeling still lurked in the baronet's breast when the bishop had reached that goal "where the wicked cease from troubling and the weary are at rest." When, saith the baronet, "he translated the Old Testament into the Welsh tongue, he had the benefit and help of Bishop Davies' and William Salesbury's works, who had done a great part thereof; yet he carried the name of all."[1]

When King James I. uttered his pithy sentiment, "No bishop, no king," at the time the leading men of the two Protestant parties held their conference at Hampton Court, whose only good fruit was the translation of the Bible which we now use, the great translator of the same sacred volume into the British tongue rested from his labours, and slept with his fathers. Yet to this day, our country, with much truth, however much shame, may say of this faithful soldier of the Cross what Wolfe sang in honour of the brave soldier of the battle-field,[2]

"Slowly and sadly we laid him down
From the field of his fame, fresh and gory.
We carved not a line, and we raised not a stone,
But left him alone with his glory."

Bishop Morgan was a man governed by a

[1] Miss Angharad Llwyd's edition of the "History of the Gwydir Family."
[2] The Burial of Sir John Moore.

well-regulated mind, whose zeal for his country was not the feelings of an enthusiast, but the love of a patriot—diligent in the discharge of his duties, conscientious in the care of his church, charitable and benevolent in his deeds, and whose incomparable piety shone above all other qualities, and reflected honour and lustre upon every action of his life.

What D'Alembert speaks so honourably in praise of Fenelon and Massillon[1]—two eminently pious prelates of France—can with truth be endorsed respecting Bishop Morgan. He died, as every bishop ought to die, without money and without debts. He was a good man, a great scholar, and "an Israelite indeed, in whom there was no guile."

Towards the latter end of his life we may safely say that his life was a life of prayer. When often he could pray no longer with his his voice, yet, by lifting up his eyes and his hands, he prayed still. When voice, hands, and eyes failed in their office, he still prayed in his heart, and continued praying as long as he continued to breathe. It was the breath of prayer that wafted his soul to the bosom of his God.

The following verses, placed under Babing-

---

[1] D'Alembert's Life of Massillon.

ton's picture, who was Bishop of Llandaff in 1591, might be well applied to Bishop Morgan, who probably succeeded him in that see :—

"Non melior, non integrior, non cultior, alter
Vir, præsul, preco, more, fide, arte fuit :
Osque probum, vultusque gravis, pectusque serenum,
Alme Deus, tales præfice ubique gregi.

EDMUND PRYS.

EDMUND PRYS, a man of very distinguished parts, was born about 1541, at a place called Gerddi Bluog, in the Parish of Llandegwyn, Merionethshire. After attaining the necessary acquirements in his native county, he entered St John's College, Cambridge, where his education was chiefly conducted, and where he obtained his degree of Master of Arts. Soon after he was ordained, he was instituted to the Rectory of Festiniog, in his native county. He did not reside in his own parish, but at Tyddyndu in the parish of Maentwrog. Probably the Rectory of Festiniog did not furnish a rectory house. In 1576 he was appointed Archdeacon of Merioneth, and as such his name and fame have descended to posterity with a fragrance of sweet-smelling savour. He was a very learned divine and a very eminent poet, and he seems to have been as much loved for the amiability of his character as he was admired for the splendour of his genius. Bishop Morgan acknowledges the debt of gratitude which he owed to Archdeacon Prys for the valuable assistance the latter had rendered him whilst engaged in translating the Bible into Welsh. The fact of his being consulted by Bishop Morgan on an undertaking of the greatest importance, which required all the skill of a philologist well versed in Greek and Hebrew—coupled with his elegant poem in Latin written in commendation of Dr John Davies' Welsh Grammar—furnishes a conclusive evidence of his great abilities as a scholar, and of his diligence in literary pursuits. His giant intellect remained unimpaired to the hour of death. His mental vigour was in full force, whilst his physical powers were encompassed with great bodily infirmities. Upon this principle Butler so ably establishes, in the first chapter of his "Analogy," the very essence of his reasoning for his assertion of the real existence of our "living powers" independent of the perishable body—the earthly house of this tabernacle. The sudden death of the late Judge Talfourd is adduced by living writers as an evidence of the truth of this principle,[1] which is evidently corroborated in the life of Edmund Prys, whose octo-

---

[1] Stock on Butler.

genarian poem has excited the admiration of most eminent scholars.[1]

To see the contrast between his bodily weakness and his mental powers was enough to create a deep and solemnly affecting impression. To see the pain-stricken countenance relax, and the contracted frame dilate, under the kindling of intellectual fire alone—to watch the infirmities of the flesh shrinking out of sight, or glorified and transfigured in the brightness of the awaking spirit—is an awful object of contemplation. Such a mastery of the purely corporeal we seldom witnessed as in this remarkably great man. His individuality was distinct to the last. For his giant mind there was nothing too great, nothing too high or too low. It glanced from earth to heaven, and from heaven to earth, with a speed and a splendour, an ease and a power, which seem almost inspired.

As a prose writer Edmund Prys was a man of great taste. His diction was full, copious, and rich—it never clogged. It ran smooth, flowing, and easy. Yet as an essayist or homilist he never distinguished himself—poetry was his domain. Indeed, the prose literature of Wales is by no means so extensive as the poetical element; it comprises, however, much

---

[1] The poem was written when he was eighty-one—he died when eighty-four.

that is valuable and curious on historical, biographical, romantic, and moral subjects. The most ancient Welsh prose possesses something of the genuis of poetry. We may say that the language itself is the language of poetry,—more so, perhaps, than any other tongue ever known, especially since the days of Goronwy Owen. The Welsh can now say, what perhaps no other nation can, that they have a poem of eight lines in their language in which there is not a single consonant. Often in two couplets there is a three-fold rhyme. This alliterative concatenation of sound possesses a peculiar facination to a Welsh ear. This poetical composition may be found in short, terse, pithy triplets, called the Triads, which are said to be of Druidic origin.'

Amongst the English public Welsh poets are little known, yet Gray does not disdain, in his "Triumphs of Owain," to paraphrase Gwalchmai's Poem on Owain, Prince of North Wales. Tennyson, in his "Idylls," grounds his enchanting poem on a Welsh legend. Mr Burrows, in his "Wild Wales," generously bestows his duo meed of praise upon a great Welsh genius. Speaking of Strata Florida,[1] the ruins of a famous old abbey in Cardiganshire, he says:— "Such broken ruins compose all which remain of

---

[1] See Morgan's "Aberytwyth, and its Vicinity."

that celebrated monastery, in which kings, saints, and mitred abbots were buried; and in which, or in whose precincts, was buried Dafydd ab Gwylim, the greatest genius of the Cimbric race, and *one of the first poets of the world.*" A great deal of Drudical mythology ran through their poetical composition even to a late period. Gruffuth Rhys, a contemporary of Edmund Prys, composed to the Deity, under the name of Hu, these following fine lines, though perhaps more applicable to the univeral Pantheism than to the God of the Christians :—

> If with small things we Hu compare,
> No smaller thing than Hu is there.
> Yet greatest of the great is He.
> Our Lord. our God of mystery;
> How swift He moves! a lucid ray,
> A sunbeam, wafts him on his way :
> He is great on land, and great on ocean,
> Of one more great I have no notion.
> 1 dread lest I should underrate
> This Being, infinitely great.

Edmund Prys was considered one of the most illustrious poets of his age, and it seemed strange that his poetical compositions—treasures so rare, and still surviving—have seen no other light than that which emanates from the pen, and not from the press. Among these numerous manuscripts are fifty-four poems of a controversial character—a paper war in poetry between him and William Cynval, who is said to have died from the effects produced by the archdeacon's poignant satirical arrows. A man whose natural disposition was gentle and generous felt some exquisite pleasure to torture his antagonist in his critical crucible. He never imagined that Cynval should ever fall a victim to his lampoonery, nor dreamed that his pen was so steeped in the poison of satire as to cause death. He enjoyed a sort of pleasurable pain—a feeling akin to love of mischief—boyish tricks, which keenly feel for any pains they inflict, yet find exquisite pleasure in the pursuit. When the news of Cynval's death reached the archdeacon's ear, the full truth flashed on his mind like lightning, which swept its course with terrible speed, but whose course is strewed with ruins. The archdeacon's conscience smote him. His playful satire had tasted the bitterness of remorse. He was much affected, and the elegy he composed on the occasion is full of the most touching pathos, a heart touched with grief —such grief so tender, so sensitive, as true friendship experiences when her best and highest feelings are deeply wounded,—David grieving for Absalom.

The fame of the archdeacon's name is perhaps after all more warmly cherished by his countrymen as the author of the Welsh metrical version of the Psalms, which for upwards of two centuries have been consecrated in the praises of successive generations, and sung a thousand times in every church and chapel throughout the Principality. It has grown with their growth, and strengthened with their strength. William Myddelton[1] (Gwilym Canoldref) had, before the Archdeacon, composed an elegant version of the Psalms, in the higher kind of Welsh metres. This work Myddelton finished when out in the West Indies, 1595. It was first published in 1603; and a second edition, after the lapse of more than two centuries, (1827) was re-issued under auspicious patronage;[2] yet, notwithstanding its higher strain, and all other merits it possessed, it never gained the popularity wherewith Edmund Prys' version is generally regarded.

Many attempts have been unsuccessfully made to *improve* Edmund Prys' unharmonious construction and imperfect rhyme; but it is like putting a new piece to an old garment, which in many instances makes the rent worse. In every instance it only makes a patchwork, and in no instance does it increase our veneration for its melody and poetry. Wordsworth's poetical sense recognized such faults in Keble's,

---

[1] He was an elder brother to Sir Hugh Myddelton.
[2] Rev. Walter Davies.

yet, with all such faults, "The Christian Year" was Wordsworth's great delight. Such sentiments we endorse respecting the archdeacon's version. With all its rhythmical faults we love it dearly, nay, perhaps the very faults constitute a peculiarity whose absence we associate with that feeling which the organ of taste realizes when the palate assures us that the dish, however delicious, has lost its flavour. Hymns vary, —some are remarkably sweet, some indifferent, some rubbish. In all we recognize a man's hand, but in Edmund Prys' Psalms, if there is no sweetness, there is good substance; if there is no rhyme, there is still good matter. As we turn from the best work of devotion—whether it be Thomas A'Kempis, Jeremy Taylor, S. Bernard, or Fenelon—with unabated joy to the Psalms of David, so with the same feelings of pleasure and delight we turn from our sweetest hymns to read the Psalms of Edmund Prys. There is nothing in them of an ephemeral character. They have stood the test of two centuries, and still possess their full flavour. As long as the Church will breathe their spirit, the spirit of true devotion will inspire her mission.

BISHOP PARRY.

RICHARD PARRY was the son and heir of John Parry, Esq., Pwllhalog, Denbighshire, and is said to have been born at Ruthin about the year 1560. His early education was entrusted to the care of Camden, who succeeded Dr Edward Grant as head master of Westminster school, a place where a host of the aristocratic youths of this country first imbibe the elements of classical education. Yet whatever distinction may be generally attached to this aristocratic seminary, Camden's name derives no distinction from that position. The sentinel on his guard is scarcely noticed by the common soldiers, but if during his watch he achieves any daring deed, he is no longer an unknown character. Westminster school conferred no honours on Camden's memory, but his works written during his mastership have immortalized his name. His "Grammactices Grecæ institutio Compendiaria, in usum Regiæ scholæ Westmonasteriensis," was received in all the public schools in England as a standard authority of that time. He was also the author of several works which gained much celebrity in their day, but Camden's Britannia" outshines all his other works, and generations yet unborn will not cease to admire its fame. What Pausanias was to Greece, Camden is to Great Britain. Under this distinguished scholar Richard Parry commenced his classical career, and it appears that he made good use of his time and talents; for when he was only nineteen years of age, he was elected student of Christ Church, Oxford, 1579. It is difficult to ascertain, at the present time, with what honours his College recognized his literary attainments; but from his rapid promotion in the Church, and the recognition wherewith his king rewarded his abilities, he was regarded as a man whose talents were of no mean order. From the time Parry left College until the year 1592, when he was instituted to the vicarage of Gresford, and also made Chancellor of Bangor Cathedral, his career seems buried in some obscurity, and the researches of the learned are no longer likely to remove the doubts which the accumulated mist of two centuries have only tended to intensify. Some strongly maintain, that at this time Richard Parry was the headmaster of Ruthin Grammar School; others would lead us to conclude that he was only employed in the capacity of a second master at this institution. It is, however, evident, that he was connected in some manner with the school, which honoured his talents, and recognized his authority.

During this time party spirit ran high in the kingdom, and few feigned to disguise their creed. Mary Stuart, the beautiful Queen of Scotland, was now a prisoner at Fotheringay Castle, under the watchful surveillance of her jealous cousin. Mary's crimes we much regret, but Mary's cruel fate we deeply deplore. Mary was a Romanist, Elizabeth was a Protestant. All in whom existed a hankering after the Romish religion cried shame on Mary's imprisonment, and in no mild terms condemned and cursed the intolerance of the Protestant faith. Few perhaps supported Elizabeth's views with regard to her conduct towards her cousin, but in a religious point of view, it made the breach wide, and the line of demarcation distinct. Those who were half and half before, were now on one side or the other. Few maintained a neutral ground. Richard Parry was not idle in the scene. It is not known whose cause he espoused, but it is well known whose creed he embraced. He was not a partisan to any political party, much less a party to any secret plots, but he was a staunch supporter of the Reformed Church, and a zealous lover of God's truth. Long before he had obtained his Doctor's degree in 1598, and long before he had been made Dean of Bangor in 1599, he had made the Word of God the sole object of his studies, and the sole charter of his life. He was, in the full force of the expression, a truly good man. Whether we regard him as a scholar, a gentleman, or a Christian, we behold in him a perfect model. When the pious Bishop Morgan (in 1604) rested from his labours, and slept amongst his predecessors at St Asaph, King James I.[1] immediately fixed upon Dean Parry as a singularly qualified person to succeed an eminently pious prelate. Morgan and Parry were men of singularly kindred dispositions. Their lives seemed consecrated to the same service, and their studies were pursued to the

[1] Much to the King's credit he appointed, just about the same time, Lewis Bayley, D.D., native of Carmarthen, to the Bishopric of Bangor. Dr Bayley is best known as the author of a very remarkable small treatise, called "The Practice of Piety, directing a Christian how to walk that he may please God." It was translated into Welsh and French, and at one time so great was its popularity that some apprehensions were entertained that by many Bishop Bayley's little treatise was regarded as of equal authority with the Bible. Scarcely had its pious author been an hundred years in his grave before the fifty-seventh edition of this unequalled little work came out from the press.

same end. Morgan translated the whole Bible, Parry revised the whole work; and the edition which Parry revised continues to remain the standard version of the Welsh Bible to this day.

Bishop Parry was eminently qualified to undertake so important a work, which he so creditably discharged; and his name as a patriot and a Christian will never fail to excite the admiration of every Welshman's heart, when he learns that this good prelate undertook such onerous responsibility solely for the benefit of his own poor countrymen. This Bible, which was printed in 1620, appeared in folio, and the variations which Bishop Parry introduced seem to effect such an improvement upon its predecessor, that doubts were once entertained whether it should be called a new version. Respecting the difference between the revision by Bishop Parry and the original by Bishop Morgan, the former says:—" Quædam cum precessoris laude retinui, quædam in Dei nomine mutavi atque sic compegi, ut et hic sit $αμφι\-δοξομενου$ $Παραδειγμα$, et dictu sit difficile, num vetus an nova, Morgani an mea, dicenda sit versio."

Bishop Parry presided over the see of St Asaph for nearly twenty years, and resided during the whole of that period in the pretty picturesque parish of Dyserth, about two miles' distance from St Asaph. The scenery in this parish is extremely rich, romanatic, and lovely. Its river, with its foaming fall in the centre of the village, winding its course through the vicarage grounds; its sweet shadowy glens with its steep perpendicular peaks, its neat looking village, with its Swiss looking cottages, bear such beautiful features as are not often seen, and are seldom surpassed. The same house where lived and died the good Bishop Parry is now worthily occupied by the respected incumbent of the parish. Before the bishop's death, he had bequeathed a portion of his property for ever towards the maintenance of poor scholars at Jesus College, Oxford, born either at Ruthin, or anywhere in the diocese of St Asaph.[1] After his death a concio ad clerum appeared as his work, and published in his name. He was buried in his own cathedral, 1623, and his remains share the same fate as his predecessor, no monument marks his resting place, and no inscription relates his good deeds, or chronicles his happy death.

Bishop Parry was one of those eight eminent prelates, natives of Wales, who in succession filled the see of St Asaph; and if that custom of electing natives to vacant bishoprics had ever since prevailed, the old British race would never have been so alienated from the old British Church.

[1] Ruthin was not then in the diocese of St Asaph.

BISHOP GRIFFITH.

George Griffith, whether we regard him as a scholar, a tutor, a preacher, or a bishop, was a very distinguished personage. He was a native of a remote part of Carnarvonshire, where its shore is washed by the sea, and its mountain peaks stretch to the clouds. As a youth he was very clever and promising; as a man he was distinguished and great.

How nearly George Griffith was related to Edmund Griffith, who just about the same time was Bishop of Bangor, or to Syr Rhys Griffith, whose son Sir Piers Griffith[1] so distinguished himself in the time of Queen Elizabeth when the Spanish Armada threatened the invasion of our shores, cannot now be ascertained with that degree of certainty which would enable us

[1] Sir Rhys Griffith is named by Queen Elizabeth in relation to Caerwys Eistedfod held 1568.—See Pennant's Tour in Wales.—Vol. II., p. 89.

to record as facts things which only exist among the remnants of tradition. That they sprang all from the same stock is not improbable; that George Griffith was the son of a very respectable family is unquestionable; and that they were all natives of Carnarvonshire, springing from the same spot,[1] is a well-known fact.

George Griffith went to Oxford at an early age, and was educated at Westminster College; and when he was only eighteen years of age he was elected student of Christ Church, where, in due course, he became very eminent as a tutor, and very popular as a preacher. His lectures were eminently instructive, and his preaching powerful and attractive. He could bring the most profound truths within the reach of the most ordinary understanding. His delivery was graceful and impressive, animated by a latent fire peculiar to the Celtic race. His voice possessed remarkable sweetness and compass, and its singing tones produced a peculiar spell. In 1629 he was appointed chaplain to Dr John Owen, Bishop of St Asaph, and obtained his doctor's degree when he was only thirty-five years of age. It is not unlikely that George Griffith during his residence at Oxford became acquainted with another Dr John Owen, who, though bearing

---

[1] Perrhyn—near Tremadoc.

the same name, and a contemporary of the bishop, was a very different character. He was a warm supporter of Oliver Cromwell, and an unflinching advocate of Independency. Whilst Bishop Owen was imprisoned in the Tower, and old Milles, who kept the post-office of St Asaph, lived in his house and sold his wine, kept his oxen in his church, fed his calves in the bishop's throne, and used the font as a horse-trough, Dr John Owen was promoted to the deanery of Christ Church, Oxford. He preached before Parliament the first day after the execution of Charles I., and enjoying the Protector's smile, accompanied him to Ireland. As during the seasons of great floods, when rivers overflow their banks, it is difficult to measure their wonted channels, so in times of anarchy and rebellion, when excitement and party spirit run high, it is not easy to estimate a man's true character. Since Dr John Owen believed himself to be actuated by right motives, our province is not to dissect cases of conscience; and although his character is differently represented, according to the bias of the writer, yet all admit that he was a great historian, a perfect master of the Latin, Greek, and Hebrew languages, well skilled in polemical divinity, and well read in the civil law. Wood, to whom he was particularly obnoxious, bears testimony, from his own personal knowledge, to his great learning and gentlemanly deportment. "He was," saith he, "a person well skilled in the tongues, Rabinnical learning, Jewish rites and customs; that he had a great command of his English pen, and was one of the most genteel and fairest writers who have appeared against the Church of England. His personage was proper and comely, and he had a very graceful behaviour in the pulpit, an eloquent elocution, a winning and insinuating deportment, and could, by the persuasion of his oratory, in conjunction with some other outward advantages, move and win the affections of his admiring auditory, almost as he pleased." As a man we have no inclination to discuss his merits, or pursue his chequered course; but as a Welshman we venture to say that he was the most voluminous writer that ever was born on Welsh soil, or ever sprang from a Celtic tribe. He was the author of seven volumes in folio, twenty volumes in quarto, and thirty volumes in octavo. Owen foresaw the Restoration, and provided against the event; and when Dr John Owen, Bishop of St Asaph, had been restored to his peaceful possessions in Wales, after his sufferings and imprisonments, Dr John Owen, the Puritan, had retired to Stadham, in Oxfordshire, an estate which he had purchased during the rebellion.[1]

George Griffith not only witnessed all these scenes, but largely shared in all the calamities and sufferings which a state of anarchy and rebellion must invariably entail. His chaplaincy had now ceased. The revenues attached to his canonry at St Asaph, which he had obtained in 1631, were now enjoyed by such men as old Milles, the St Asaph postmaster, or Watkin Jones,[2] the Glamorganshire sequestrator. He had exchanged the rectory of Llanvechan, and was ousted from the rectory of Llandrinio, but he is generally supposed to have retained possession of Llanymynach. He was not cowed under these frowning signs of the times, nor was he afraid to speak his mind when his person, no less than his property, was often in great danger. Vavasor Powell, a native of Radnorshire,—who acted in the capacity of a curate in Shropshire (though no proof has ever been adduced that he had been ordained), and

---

[1] There were two Bishops, respectively bearing the name of Owen, viz., Bishop of St Asaph, and Bishop of Llandaff, both very eminently pious men, imprisoned at the same time, and for the same cause.

[2] Watkin Jones, living in the diocese of Llandaff, who was a strict Anabaptist at Mynyddyslwyn, and a zealous Presbyterian at Bedwas, after he had failed in breaking a very fine stone font, used it, like old Milles of St Asaph, as a trough to water his horses.

who afterwards embraced the tenets of Anabaptism, which sect at the time was very unpopular in Wales, in consequence of which he retired to London, where he attracted some notice as a preacher, and became a well-known character,—had now returned into Wales, and being protected by the "Act for the Propagation of the Gospel in Wales," in which he was named a commissioner, he was fully determined that not a stone upon another be left of the old established temple in the land. Dr Griffith not only wrote a modest reply to Vavasor Powell's bold challenge, but confronted him face to face. We can partly imagine in what spirit these controversialists met; but with what decorum the disputation was conducted, and with what result it ended, we have no materials for information,—probably like most public disputations on religious controversy, which seldom produce any conviction, but often tend to widen the breach. Both disputants create a party, whose respective voices applaud their respective champions. Dr Griffith, however, published his own animadversions, not on the issue, but on the imperfect manner in which the whole disputation had been narrated.[1] It evi-

---

[1] It is admitted that Dr Griffith was a man of great contro-

dently produced no effect on Vavasor Powell's zeal, for he proceeded to eject a number of the clergy out of their livings, out of which he not only had £100 per annum, but exacted enormous sums from the same sources. It is said that he preached the Gospel with great zeal and success in every nook and corner of Wales. How could the preaching of the Gospel, which breathes love and charity, be made consistent with the heartless manner in which he deprived many a poor family of their bread, leaving them destitute of a home, sounds paradoxical to our sense of honour and sentiments of religion. His admirers declare that he did much good. His detractors protest that he did much harm. In a certain sense, probably, he accomplished both ends in some degree. In his itinerant journeys, he was joined by the famous Walter Cradock, a great Puritan, but not a republican; however, they soon parted. One was in favour of a republic, the other was in favour of monarchy. It is singular to observe that the Christian religion is not exempt from such ruptures. Paul and Barnabas separated on grounds of personal feeling. Cradock and Powell separated on political grounds. After the Restoration, Vavasor Powell was cast from prison to prison, until at last he

---

versial powers, accurate in his statements, acute in his reasoning, and rigid in his deductions.

died within their precincts. If he acted cruelly in ejecting the clergy—and it is to be regretted that his zeal for what he believed to be the truth was not tempered by more of a charitable and gentle spirit—yet it is a sad spectacle to see an old man being made the tool of revenge. If his conduct is to be blamed, his persecution is to be deplored—one inflicted injury, the other inflicted death. Dr Griffith, whilst he contested every inch of ground with his zealous Puritan opponent, conducted himself throughout as becometh a man, wise, good, and great. He employed no epithet unbecoming a gentleman, and stooped to no meanness unbecoming a man. The caustic sarcasms, wielded with no ordinary dexterity, issued from a more poignant pen than that of Dr Griffiths. An explanation is here necessary, otherwise a confusion may ensue. Vavasor Powell and his adherents were vigorously attacked by another able writer of the name of Griffiths. This was Alexander Griffiths, the author of " Mercurius Cambro Britannicus, Strena Vavasoriensis, or a hue and cry after Vavasor Vowell, Metroplitan of the itinerants, and one of the executioners of the Gospel, by colour of the late Act for the Propagation thereof in Wales." This Alexander Griffiths, after the Restoration, was the vicar of Glasbury in Breconshire, whilst Dr George Griffith was, in the year 1660, promoted to the see of **St Asaph**. After Dr Griffiths had retired from the field of controversy he devoted his great powers to the services of the Church, and the first work which engaged his attention was the translation of the New Common Prayer Book into Welsh. The execution of this work, however the translation may appear here and there somewhat stiff, not possessing that easy elastic flow of which the resources of the Welsh tongue are so abundant, displays great skill and judgment, and possesses unquestionable merits. Soon after his elevation to the see of St Asaph we find him an active member of Convocation, concurring entirely in drawing up the Act of Conformity, and making certain alterations in the Book of Common Prayer; and it is generally thought that the Form for Adult Baptism was Bishop Griffith's own composition. Many may deem such forms unnecessary, but Dr Griffith regarded them highly expedient, before everything in the service of the Church could be done " decently and in order." Those who disregard all forms, nevertheless conduct their religious services in an extremely formal manner. We need not despise forms, which are resources of great help, but we should avoid formality, which is the essence of death. It is a custom in many parts of Wales—a custom which should more universally prevail—on the death of any person in the neighbourhood, to hold religious services at that house on the eve before burial, and it is said that Bishop Griffith composed a most beautiful service, singularly appropriate for such an occasion. However, like his Discourses on the Sacrament, and other sermons, it is feared that this night's watch liturgy was not published for many years after the bishop's death, when its savour was lost under the dust of years. During the short space of six years which Bishop Griffith presided over the see of St Asaph, he laboured hard to promote the interest of the Church, and spread the spirit of Christianity; and the principles of religion which he so much cultivated in life, shed their hallowed influence on the hour of his death. As the autumn leaves fell to the ground, this good Christian bishop was carried to his grave. He died November 1666, and was buried in the choir of his own cathedral.[1]

[1] Williams, in his "Dictionary of Eminent Welshmen," says that one of Bishop Griffith's daughters married John Middleton, Esq., Gwaenynog, where the bishop's portrait is still preserved.

JOHN DAVIES, D.D.

This great man was born at Llanferres, in the county of Denbigh, about the year 1570. Llanferres, which lies midway between Ruthin and Mold, and through which the river Alun pursues its course from the mountains of Denbighshire to the estuary of the Dee, is celebrated from being the parish in which Wilson, the great landscape painter, lived, who might well be styled the Claude of Wales. Llanferres church is dedicated to St Berres (Britius), disciple of St Martin the Hungarian, towards the close of the fourth century. The present edifice owes its existence mostly to the bounteous liberality of Mrs Catharine Jones, Colomendy, who at the time the church was last restored, was the owner of that picturesque residence. Pennant, in his "Tours through Wales," says:—"The east end of the old church (Llanferres) was repaired in 1650, by Dr John Davies, the author of the Welsh-Latin-Dictionary, a most skilful antiquary, native of this parish."

John Davies' father, though he carried on the trade of a weaver at Llanferres, was, nevertheless, respectably connected,[1] and not improbably a man in good circumstances. The trade has since fallen into disrepute, and at the present day is almost become extinct, even in Wales. But weavers of the early part of the sixteenth century, were the woollen manufacturers of our country, and the gigantic cotton mills of Manchester were not then in existence. The general wearing apparel of both male and female, was, at a much later date, manufactured generally in country places, of woollen materials.

John Davies was, at an early age, sent to Ruthin school, where his education was conducted under the care of Dr Richard Parry.[2] Between master and pupil there sprang up such close intimacy and sincere friendship, which grew with their years, and which, we hope, did not cease with their death. For love is stronger than death. When he was only nineteen years of age he entered Jesus College, Oxford; and it is not improbable but that at this time he cultivated the friendship of the learned Bishop Andrewes, than whom a more eminent prelate never lived, and who was then a scholar of the same College. Here Davies

---

[1] See Dwn's "Heraldic Visitation through Wales."
[2] See Bishop Parry's Life.

remained four years, and gained considerable reputation for learning and industry, for he knew that diligence and perseverance are elements essential to success in pursuits of study. Many great geniuses have laid waste their talent through want of culture, whilst ordinary intellects have attained high eminence by diligent application. He now, in 1593, returned to his native country; and though he had lost sight of his dear old *alma mater*, he never lost sight of his books. In order to prevent any desultory reading, from which real advantage is seldom gained, he arranged his studies, which he pursued with no languid vigour, under three heads, —Theology, Languages, and Antiquities. The Welsh tongue and the antiquities of Wales were first to occupy his attention, but as his acquaintance with these native subjects grew familiar, he extended his field of operation to other languages as well as other countries. He was admitted into deacon's orders, and in the same year as Bishop Morgan died, he was promoted to the Rectory of Mallwyd, in Merionethshire, and at the same time was appointed chaplain to Bishop Parry, his former tutor at Ruthin school. Mallwyd stands at the upper end of a narrow but sweet valley, whose sides seem chained to a range of lofty mountains, and fastened at the end to a stupendous abrupt perpendicular peak, under which stands Mallwyd church. The river Dovey, which enriches and runs through the valley, makes the whole look as if let down from Heaven, fastened at the four corners, surpassing in natural beauty the hanging gardens of Babylon. In this sequestered spot, surrounded by mountains and mountain shepherds, the very recluse of nature, lived Dr Davies for forty years, with perhaps one intermittent occasion, when he went to Oxford, and was admitted of Lincoln College, as reader of Bishop Lombard's sentences. He had now become a very distinguished man; and promotions, which would have turned and intoxicated a weaker head, did not ruffle his equilibrium, except that in the same proportion as his means increased, increased also his liberality and generosity. In 1612 he was made canon of St Asaph, in 1613 he had the rectory of Llanymowddwy, in 1615 he had the sinecure rectory of Darowen, in 1616 he obtained his doctor's degree, and 1617 he was appointed to the prebend of Llanefydd.

After these whirling promotions had ceased—allowing a little time for the sediment to settle, and the water to become once more clear—he began to publish to the world the result of nearly twenty years' private study. In 1620 appeared the Welsh Bible, in revising which he rendered

Bishop Parry most material and invaluable assistance. It is said of the English Bible, considerable portion of which was at the same time revised by the famous Bishop Andrewes, in consequence of his acquaintance with language and divinity, that its "marvellous English and uncommon beauty" excite the admiration even of those who refuse to adopt it. The praise which was so justly bestowed upon the English edition, the conjoint labour of Bishop Andrewes and those appointed with him, might with equal justice be applied to the Welsh edition, the conjoint labour of Bishop Parry and Dr Davies. Again, the next year (1621), Dr Davies published his Welsh Grammar entitled, "Antiquæ Linguæ Britannicæ Rudimentæ," a second edition of which, under the able editorship of the late Rev. Henry Parry, Vicar of Llanasa, Flintshire, was published in 1809, not much less than two centuries after its original prototype. This excellent work, written in Latin, displays an intimate acquaintance with the rudimental elements of the Celtic tongue. About ten years after he published his Grammar, he published his Dictionary, bearing the title of "Antiquæ Linguæ Britannicæ Dictionarium, duplex." This consists of two parts, and would look better in two volumes. The first being Welsh and Latin the second being

Latin and Welsh, which latter part was only revised by Dr Davies. Its actual author was Dr Thomas Williams, a learned lexicographer and physician; and it is stated by those who have examined the original, consisting of three quarto volumes in the Hengwrt MSS., that the edition revised by Dr Davies is no more than a bare index to Williams' Lexicon Latino-Britannicum, which is the result of deep research; and its publication, even at the present day, would add to the riches of our philological treasury. Dr Williams sacrificed the interest of his profession to his tastes for literary pursuits, and it is much to be regretted that his works, on various subjects, should have shared the same fate as his Dictionary, which remains, even to this day, in their original manuscript form.

In the same year as Dr Davies published his Dictionary, which remained in great repute for about two hundred years, until superseded by that of Dr Owen Pughe, he published also his translation of Parson's " Christian Resolution." [1] This was a very popular work amongst all classes

---

[1] Dr John Davies' " Christian Resolution" was translated by Owen Jones, called " Dyhewyd-y-Cristion." This famous Welshman, Owen Jones, was a native of Llanfihangel-Glyn-y-Myfir, Denbighshire. He went to London at an early age, and accumulated an early fortune, which he employed

and denominations in Wales, especially during the time, which soon followed, when our country was convulsed through its very centre. This valuable little volume proved an anchor to many a soul. It is to his diligent pen we are also indebted for a translation into Welsh of the Articles of Religion, which, however valuable, are little known except amongst the clergy.

In the Bodleian library and the British Museum are preserved, in MSS., many of Dr Davies' collections of Welsh poems and proverbs. Circumstances offered Dr Davies rare opportunities for enriching his collections with such materials. Adjoining his native parish lies Llanarmon-in-yale[1]—a parish remarkable for its mounds, supposed to be the graves of our Welsh chieftains. Here lived Gyrys, who made the first collection of Welsh proverbs, known by the name of Madwaith hen Gyrys o Ial, or the good work of old Gyrys of Yale. The township of Erryrys, in this parish, formerly called Treryris, in all probability derives its name from Gyris, the great collector of Welsh proverbs. The treasure-house of Old Gyris, the proverbialist, could scarcely have been unknown for literary purposes. The Myfyrian Archaiology, a work of inestimable value, is so called after the name of his native parish.

[1] See an excellent history of this parish in the Gwyliedydd (1832).—page 257.

to Dr Davies, whose early days were spent in the same neighbourhood, whose taste and feelings were in harmony with such pursuits, and in an age when Welsh proverbs were better known—and I fear more appreciated—than the Welsh Bible or the Welsh Prayer Book. Dr Davies is said to have been a man "well versed in the history and antiquities of his nation, and in the Greek and Hebrew languages a most exact critic, an indefatigable searcher into ancient scripts, and well acquainted with curious and rare authors."

In consequence of his charity, his humane feelings, and, above all, his great learning, coupled with his efforts to improve the temporal advantages of his neighbours, by building bridges, as well as his exertions in preaching the Christian faith, he was in his lifetime much eulogized by the poets of his age, and after his death he was canonized in the metrical effusion of the same fraternity.

He was married, but left no issue; when therefore he died, our hopes were buried in his grave. And though no descendants honour his name, still we possess more lasting monuments which record his deeds. He died at Mallwyd rectory, May 15, 1644, and was buried in his own church. On his tombstone was inscribed the following, which has since been effaced by the hand of time:—

"Johannes Davies, S. T. P., Rector Ecclesiæ Parochialis de Mallwyd, Obiit 15 die Maii, et sepultus fuit 19, A.D. 1644, in virtutis potius quam nominis memoria."

Whilst our intellect cannot inherit his name, may our hearts imitate his virtues!

RHYS PRICHARD.

Rhys Prichard, an eminent divine and sincere Christian, was born in the neighbourhood of Llandovery, about the year 1579. The history of his early career is to a great extent buried amongst the ruins of tradition, yet it is known that his father held a respectable position, and had a large family. Rhys was his eldest son, who, at an early age, was sent to Brecon Grammar School. Some contend that Prichard was brought up at Carmarthen Grammar School; but to refute such notions, it is only necessary to state that Carmarthen Grammar School was founded by Dr Morgan Owen, who was Bishop of Llandaff, and a contemporary and an intimate friend of Rhys Prichard. In 1597 he was sent to Jesus College, Oxford, and about this time it is related of him that he was much addicted to the sin most prevalent in his time, and which, as is too well known, mostly occurs to such as delight to frequent the public-house. His general companion, which everywhere followed him like a faithful dog, was a fine he-goat. On one occasion he induced this poor animal to drink of the same pot as his master. The effect produced upon the boon companion can be well imagined. When his master saw him next day, lying full length on the ground, his pitiable condition excited his sympathy; he raised him from the ground, caressed and coaxed him, but nothing would induce him ever after to follow Prichard to the public-house. Prichard's reflections produced very great change. He deemed himself worse than the beasts that perish, and from the effects produced upon the creature, and his subsequent refusal to accompany his master to his haunts of carousals, Prichard was led, by Divine Providence, to repent of his former course, and to lead a new life.

Nothing is memorably known of his college career; but before he had obtained his degree of B.A., in 1602, he had been admitted into priest's orders, by John, Suffragan Bishop of Colchester.[1] In the absence of any proof to the contrary, the most reasonable way to account for such irregularities of admitting one to holy

---

[1] It appears that by an Act of Henry VIII., Colchester had been created a suffragan see, though only now an archdeaconry.

orders before obtaining his degree, is to attribute it to his good conduct, learning, and piety. For the same year as he was ordained by the Suffragan of Colchester, he was appointed to the vicarage of Llandingad by the Bishop of St David's.[1] He was by this promotion brought back to his native place; and as it is well known that the parish of Llandingad includes the town of Llandovery, and that he resided in the latter during his lifetime, which accounts for the origin of the general appellation of the "Vicar of Llandovery."

One of the most distinguished of his parishioners was Sir George Devereux, Bart., who was an uncle to the dauntless Earl of Essex, the great favourite of Queen Elizabeth. After the earl had endured the final penalty of the law, and the whims of his imperious mistress, Sir George Devereaux[2] became the natural guardian of the young earl, to whom Vicar Prichard was appointed as his chaplain, and through whose interest he was afterwards appointed to the rectory of Llanedi, Carmarthenshire, by his majesty King James I. To this

[1] Dr Anthony Rudd.

[2] Sir George Devereaux married Joan, the daughter of Sir John Price, Brecon, who, after her husband's death, married Thomas Jones, Esq., Fountain Gate, Tregaron, the notorious *Twm Sion Catti*—the Dick Turpin of Wales.

rural retreat the vicar often resorted. His kindness and courtesy won the affections of the people, and his powerful mode of preaching attracted their deep attention. The church could not hold his congregation. He was obliged to preach in the churchyard. Dr Anthony Rudd, the excellent Bishop of St David's, rejoiced in his heart at the great success which accompanied his ministry, and, as a mark of his good pleasure, appointed Prichard Prebendary of the Collegiate Church of Brecon. This preferment, which added little to his labours, added materially to his income. As this was the last preferment conferred upon Prichard by Bishop Rudd, it may not be inappropriate to remark, that this good prelate greatly admired and encouraged all men whose preaching and practice were of the same stamp and character as that of the vicar of Llandovery. Dr Rudd, who succeeded the learned Dr Middleton, is said to have been not only a very eloquent and impressive preacher, but also very faithful and conscientious in discharging such duties as related to his office. It is related of him, that whilst preaching before Queen Elizabeth he gave great offence to Her Majesty for reminding her in his sermon that she was getting old. She soon displayed the absurdity of such notions. A miniature engraving, which could not be distinctly seen except through the medium of a magnifying glass, she read with her naked eyes. After she had thus gratified her vanity, she pardoned the doctor. This excellent prelate died at Aberglasney, an estate he had purchased in Carmarthenshire, in the year 1615, and was succeeded by Dr Richard Milborne.

About this time there was a spirit of peculiar licentiousness pervading the mass of the population; and this evil, which was encouraged by the king, occasioned such men as Prichard most *painful* feelings. It was enacted by the king, though strictly forbidden by Dr Abbot, Archbishop of Canterbury, that after divine service on Sundays the people should not be discouraged from amusing themselves in various kinds of games practised amongst them. The archbishop's spiritual restraint could not curb the spirit of the populace when such a feeling was fostered by the temporal power. This induced the vicar to compose several kinds of spiritual songs, which he directed to be sung in the church. His songs produced the desired effect, and soon induced those engaged in the games in the churchyard, to join in praise in the church.

In the composition of these songs he adopted an easy colloquial style, calculated to enlist the feelings of the whole mass of the populace, and not a few of the learned. The harmonious metrical verses of the Psalms of Captain William Middleton, edited by Mr Thomas Salesbury, were constructed in strict conformity with all the rules of grammar and the license of poetry. It excited the admiration of the learned few, but it never reached the heart of the general mass. Middleton (Gwylim Canoldref) adopted a style in strict conformity with the *letter* of poetry. Prichard, regardless of the rules, and adopting an easy style, breathed the language of the voice and heart, which created an enthusiasm which, after the lapse of centuries, remains unabated. This is what he says :—

> "Ni cheisiais ddim Cywreinwaith,
> Ond mesur esmwyth perffaith,
> Hawdd ei ddysgu ar fyr o dro,
> Gan bawb a'i clywo deirgwaith."

It is evident that Mr Prichard had been soon married after he became settled at Llandovery, but of his wife nothing is known except that her name was Gwenllian, and that they had one son. His name was Samuel, and like the Samuel of old he had been early consecrated to the service of God. The beautiful prayer which his father composed in verse, was for the use of his son when he was only ten years of age.

In another incomparably sweet poem, this pious father, in a graceful and touching style, pours out the deep emotions of his soul in trying to impress upon his son the duty and obligation laid upon him to lead a moral and Christian life. The son, at this time a member of Jesus College, Oxford, writes his father a long letter,[1] in which he expresses his deep regret that his "præcipitant courses should haue causde soe many stormes of vexation" to his father, and hopes "in God that his reformed life shall moue such cheerfulness of mind, that those grey haires shall re-obtain theire former lustre." Under this promise of repentance and change of life, it is probable his father allowed him to proceed, and be admitted into holy orders. And though Mr Samuel Prichard was now married to Frances, daughter of Mr Harding, Oxford, and from all accounts was a curate to his father, yet it is sad to relate that the son would not be guided by his father's counsel, but pursued his own course. When the Court was governed by a weak king, and much influenced by a licentious boon companion,[2] we can easily imagine the immorality which prevailed in the country.

[1] This letter alluded to here is now in the possession of the late renowned antiquary, Rev. J. M. Traherne, Coedriglan, near Cardiff.

[2] King James I. and his favourite Buckingham.

Mr Samuel Prichard was on terms of intimate friendship with Sir Francis Lloyd, Maesyfelin, near Lampeter. This gentleman is said to have been steeped in all the profligacy, licentiousness, and recklessness which the vices and sins of that age could be guilty of. Yet at this man's house Mr Samuel Prichard was a frequent guest, and if his host did not become his actual murderer, he became the means whereby young Prichard met an untimely death, and hurled into a premature grave. Many reasons are assigned for this foul deed, but jealousy is the most probable cause. Sir Francis Lloyd, though married to a daughter of John, Earl of Carberry, yet had several children by a woman named Bridget Leigh, from Carmarthen, whom he publicly treated as his concubine; and in all probability the quarrel originated from a feeling of mortal jealousy arising from this illicit source. Mr Samuel Prichard is said to have been smothered between two feather beds, put across his own horse in a woolsack, and thrown over a narrow bridge (which has long since been replaced by an iron bridge leading into the town of Llandovery), into the river Towy, just as if he had fallen accidentally off his horse, and drowned in the river. When the horse, without its rider, reached home, the vicar, under a feeling of well-grounded suspicion, intuitively apprehending his son's fate, is said to have uttered, *inpromptu,* the following malediction :—

> " Melldith Duw fo a'r Maesyfelin,[1]
> Ar bob carreg a phob Gwreiddyn
> Am daflu blodau tre' Llanddyfri
> Ar ei ben i Dywi i foddi !"

Vicar Prichard was a man of undaunted spirit, a brave Christian hero, and, in the full force of the expression, a truly good man. When the great plague was raging in London, the good-hearted vicar left his quiet country town, and hastened to the scene of death. Unmindful of

---

[1] Maesyfelin was the property of Sir Marmaduke Lloyd, a well known judge, and a friend of Vicar Prichard. His father was Thomas Lloyd, Treasurer of St David's Cathedral, and his mother was the daughter of Dr Marmaduke Middleton, who was Bishop of St David's for upwards of thirty years. Sir Francis Lloyd was therefore Bishop Middleton's great grandson, and his mother was a Miss Stedman, Strata Florida, Cardiganshire. There is now a monument in the church of Mynachlog Ystrad Flur, to one Ann Stedman. The family is extinct, but the name is still borne by one or two miners in that neighbourhood. It is generally believed that the vicar's curse fell heavily upon Maesyfelin. The house and the family fell to wreck and ruin, and it is traditionally affirmed, that in consequence of taking materials from Maesyfelin to build Ffynnon Bedr, the latter shared the same fate.

> " A mynych yr ych oi iau,
> A bawr lawr ei balyrau.
> D. D. Cwymp Ffynnon Bedr.

any danger, and regardless of any contact, he rushed, like Aaron of old, amongst the suffering, the dying, and the dead. And whilst the great and wealthy were holding their Parliament in Oxford, poor Vicar Prichard was working night and day to alleviate the distresses of London. At the time when this eminent Christian pastor had left his flock and his parish in Wales, to visit the plague-stricken district of London, Bishop Laud took the opportunity to leave London to visit his see in Wales. Dr Laud, who had been elevated to this dignified position through the influence of Archbishop Williams, to whom he is said to have requited this kind office with a piece of courtesy singularly ungracious, was not a man whose religious sentiments were of a kindred nature with the vicar's religious views; but the vicar's name and fame exercised such powerful influence that he could not be left unnoticed without committing an act of the gravest indiscretion; and when Mr Baillie resigned the Chancellorship of St David's, Laud promoted Prichard to the same office, being, it appears, instituted in St David's by an arrangement of Bishop Beck, 1287, and an office next in dignity, position, and power to the bishop himself. After this promotion, the venerable vicar used to preach occasionally at the Cathedral, but the spacious building afforded no adequate room to hold the vast congregation that flocked therein, which caused him to procure a moveable pulpit, placed in the churchyard, whence his message could reach every ear. For this, and other seeming irregularities, a charge was preferred against him, to which he alludes in the following verse :—

> " Ti ro'ist gennad i estroniaid,
> Lwyr amcanu ddifa f'enaid,
> A'r sawl nad wy'n nabod etto,
> Lwyr amcanu fy anrheithio."

Under these circumstances he committed his case into God's hands, he sought not the counsel of the wise, and solicited not the support of the great, but simply relying upon Him whose he was and whom he served; and without furnishing us with any particulars, or the mode he effected his deliverance, he gives all the glory of his escape, *in his next canto*, to God, which he expresses in a beautiful poetical strain in the following verse :—

> " Helodd angel i'm dad-ddrysu,
> Rhoes ei Ysbryd i'm diddanu,
> Taenodd droswy 'i aden hyfryd,
> Ac am tynnodd o'm holl ofid."

The Rev. John Bulmer, in his preface to his English work called, " The Beauties of the

Vicar of Llandovey," refers to him as one of the Puritan poets of Wales. If Mr Bulmer implied Non-conformity, he has erred much, for the vicar, to his dying day, was a staunch Churchman. This is satisfactorily proved by the evidence of contemporary writers, who, on friendly terms with the vicar, though Nonconformists themselves, bear ample testimony to his being a true son of the Church. The vicar lived in troublous times, and to many incidents which occurred therein, he frequently alludes in his poetry. The failure attending the matrimonial project which induced the king's son, accompanied by Buckingham, to go to Spain, was a source of a new life in his heart. The prince's subsequent marriage with a French Roman Catholic princess, he treats with feelings of undisguised regret. The intestine broils between Episcopalians and Puritans, which so disturbed the peace of the Church, and marred the cause of his Master, bowed down his spirits. A new publication of the Bible in Welsh, at five shillings per copy, through the noble efforts of Middleton and Heylin,[1] he regarded with the

---

[1] Sir Thomas Middleton was the third son of Richard Middleton who guarded Denbigh Castle in the reign of Edward VI., Mary, and Elizabeth. They were three brothers; and no three men ever reflected greater lustre upon their country. William was a famous seaman, and a rare Welsh poet. Hugh

same feelings of joyful enthusiasm as warms the sailor's breast when he beholds the morning's dawn. The civil war which was raging in the country was an iron which entered into his soul. When different factions were attributing certain disasters and calamities which befel his country, to different causes, he laid all to the charge of the nation's sin. At the bar of the last day our judgment shall be individually and personally. Nations as nations shall undergo no sentence; consequently, nations as nations are here often inflicted with punishment for the sins they commit. When the "Book of Plays" had been commanded to be read after divine service, some of the clergy obeyed, some refused to obey, others half obeyed, for after reading the "Book of Plays," they immediately read the fourth commandment, remarking, at the same time, that one was the word of man, and the other was the Word of God. What course Prichard pursued under these circumstances, there remains

(the well-known Sir Hugh Middleton, who brought two streams of water to London), displayed eminent engineering talents. Thomas was a Mayor of London. Heylin descended from the ancient family of Pentreheylin, in Montgomeryshire. They adopted the name of Heylin from being cupbearers to the Princess of Powys. Heylin became sheriff and alderman of London. His name is deservedly honoured amongst Welshmen for his benevolent considerations towards Wales.—See Heylin's "Life," written by Bishop Laud.

no record. We know that he viewed any desecration of this blessed day of rest as a grievous outrage upon the principles of religion, which everywhere teaches us to regard that day as a day distinctly set apart for holy and religious purposes. Much also depended upon the bishop of the diocese; and as Dr Field, who was now Bishop of St David's, did not regard the king's command on this subject with any great favour, doubtless much laxity was allowed, and what the bishop did not care to insist upon, Vicar Prichard did not care to omit. The vicar, a few years before he died, made two wills. In the first will he bequeaths almost all his property to his grandson, Rice Prichard, residing at Stroudwater, Gloucestershire; but in his second will there is no allusion to this grandson, from which it is naturally concluded that he had died in the meantime. His property was left amongst numerous relations, but mostly to Elizabeth, his grand-daughter, who was married to Thomas Mainwaring, son of Dr Roger Mainwaring, the Bishop of St David's, so well known in history as the author of the celebrated sermon on "Apostolic Obedience," for which he suffered so much persecution and imprisonment. Of his many writings, and numerous manuscripts and sermons, only "Canwyll y Cymru" and one sermon remain of Vicar

Prichard's work in our possession at the present day.

On the authority of Anthony Wood, it is stated that the venerated vicar died December, 1644, and is supposed to have been buried at Llandingad. Yet it is singular that no more than thirty-eight years after his burial, no one knew where his grave was. Dr Bull, the learned Bishop of St David's, from feelings of great attachment and respect to the memory of so eminent a servant of God, desired to be buried by his side. But such request could not be complied with, inasmuch as his resting-place was an unknown spot. Thus ends our brief sketch of one of the greatest and most popular preachers ever bred amongst the mountains of Wales, whose poetical production, which possesses such force, ease, and rhythm, and which breathes such piety, tenderness, and love, remains to this day, after the lapse of more than two hundred centuries, unmatched and incomparable, and is a source of unspeakable comfort to young and old, rich and poor, in every house, and on every hearth, wherever exists a Welshman's spirit, or wherever beats a Welshman's heart.

RESURGERIT.

GRIFFITH JONES.

GRIFFITH JONES, more generally known as Griffith Jones Llanddowrwr, was born in 1683, in the parish of Kilrhedin, Carmarthenshire. He was a very promising youth, and his early education, at the Grammar School, Carmarthen, evinced in the boy the future character of the man. However, we must candidly admit that our materials, which furnish the history of his early life, are scanty and uninteresting. He had few contemporaries as eminent men. He stood much alone in the world. The venerable old vicar of Llandovery had been well nigh half a century in his grave before he had been born, and the single-hearted, self-denying Stephen Hughes had rested from his labours when Griffith Jones was yet but five years old. Again, he was grown to be man when John Jones,[1]

---

[1] Jones was the author of several works, which, on his death, were claimed by Dawson, and placed in the Dissenters' Library, in Red Cross Street.—See Chalmers' Biographical Dictionary.

native of Carmarthen, better known, perhaps, as curate to the great Dr Young, was in his infancy. But the stately old town of Carmarthen furnished ample materials for a mind religiously disposed. In a conspicuous part in one of its many streets, there stands a peculiar looking old tree, upon whose existence the seasons of the year have long ago ceased to produce any effect. Still it has a life and language peculiarly its own; for under its shadow the good Bishop Farrar suffered martyrdom.[1] Perhaps the fire

[1] Robert Farrar, the martyred Bishop of St David's, was a Yorkshireman. When a youth, he became a canon regular of the Order of St Austin, and after some residence at Cambridge was admitted into St Mary's College, Oxford, the very nursery of that order. He was chaplain to Archbishop Cramner, and followed his Grace's example by taking to himself a wife. He was chosen prior of St Oswald's monastery in Yorkshire, and on the dissolution of that establishment by Henry VIII., in 1540, received an annual pension of £100. In 1548 he was consecrated Bishop of St. David's, and finding that a systematic spoliation of the Cathedral was in progress, set himself to check it, and accordingly ordered a commission. The form was left to the chancellor, and appeared in the old papal style, without sufficient acknowledgment of the king's supremacy. This blunder his enemies took advantage of to accuse him of a *præmunire*. An indictment was served against him, containing fifty-six charges—most of which were of the most frivolous nature. On the accession of Queen Mary he was charged with heresy, and was brought, with Hooper, Bradford, Royers, and Sanders, before Gardiner, by whom he was coarsely treated, and remanded to St David's, to be tried by Morgan, his successor. The principal charges

kindled under the bishop's stake singed its leaves, and sapped its life, but the old tree still stands and tells its own tale.[1] Such a scene, and relics of suffering and dying for the sake of true religion, must appear to a man of Griffith Jones' religious feelings, a kind of holy ground. In the year 1708 he was ordained deacon by the learned Bishop Bull, scarcely a year before that eminent prelate had been summoned to rest from his labours. Yet this short acquaintance proved immensely serviceable to Griffith Jones. For his works, wherewith Wales has

preferred against him were, that he allowed the priest to marry, denied the bodily presence in the sacrament, and the propitiatory character of the mass, refused to elevate and adore the Host, and asserted that man was justified by faith alone; but pardon was offered him on condition he would conform to the Catholic Church, but Dr Farrar refused answering, until he had evidence of the commission of Morgan. After several examinations, Dr Farrar still refused to renounce his faith, whereupon Morgan degraded him from his ecclesiastical functions, and handed him over to the sheriff for punishment. He was burned at Carmarthen on the 30th of March 1555. It is recorded that a young gentleman, named Jones, condoled with the bishop on the severity of the sentence, when he got the remarkable answer, "If you see me once stir while I suffer the pain of burning, then give no credit to those doctrines for which I die." He stood perfectly unmoved, until a ruffian, named Gravel, beat him down with a staff. It would seem certain that this prosecution against him was owing to his constancy in avowing the Protestant faith.

[1] The author believes the old tree still remains, as he last saw it some ten years ago.

been so much blessed ever since, are in a great degree owing to this circumstance, for the bishop's writings were Griffith Jones' great store house. In less than three years after he had been ordained, he was appointed to the living of Llandeilo-Abercowyn, and in a few years afterwards he was appointed to the vicarage of Llanddowrwr, where he lived and laboured for forty-four years, and whence he made himself known throughout the whole principality of Wales. If poets and bards are entitled to the title of immortality in virtue of the merits of their poetical strains, we are under no hesitation to conclude that Griffith Jones, upon far higher grounds, can establish an infinitely higher claim to that blessing, in consequence of the sincerity of his profession, which he exemplified in his life, and the purity of doctrine which he preached from the pulpit.

To the living of Llanddowrwr he was appointed by Sir John Phillips, of Picton, solely on account of his learning and piety, his great abilities as a preacher, and his watchful care as a parish priest. A friendship based upon the high principles of merits, and sustained by the noble principles of virtue, generally attracts to itself such kindred feelings as are seldom extinguished; and the vicar of Llanddowrwr had not been long his patron's friend before he was married to his patron's sister. The connection augmented his influence, and extended his usefulness. He was very zealous for his Master's cause, and very diligent in his Master's work. The Society for the Propagation of the Gospel in Foreign Parts thought him admirably adapted for an Indian missionary, and, amongst its many honourable offices, offered him a distinguished post. The distant field in a foreign land he expressed his readiness to occupy; but circumstances occurred which frustrated the design, and thus his valuable services, which would have been spent amongst a foreign race, were happily preserved for his own countrymen.

It was about this time, whilst serving the church in the parish of Llanllwch, that he became acquainted with the warm-hearted and benevolent Mrs Beavan, who is well and deservedly known in Wales by her legacy to the circulating schools throughout the whole of the principality, and which has proved of inestimable blessing, especially in years gone by, to thousands of that rising generation, who now heartily acknowledge the blessing, and reap the fruit which their benefactress so generously bestowed, and so handsomely conferred.

The originator of this school system was Mr Griffith Jones. He planted small schools in remote localities, and made a kind of an annual tour to inspect their condition, and report their progress. On these occasions he was invariably invited by the clergyman of the parish which he visited, to preach in the parish church, where crowds were seen eagerly catching the words of truth, as they hung upon his lips. These periodical visits were unflaggingly conducted for no less a period than thirty years, and were looked forward to with feelings of great joy. On these occasions Mr Jones was in the habit of publicly catechising a number of adults in the church, either on the Creed, the Lord's Prayer, the Ten Commandments, or sometimes some portion of Scripture fixed upon and prepared beforehand. This mode of instruction, sanctioned by the Church, but now almost universally neglected, proved a most effectual means of conveying religious truths, and creating religious impression.[1] It is very probable that this missionary kind of labour, which Mr Jones conducted with immense advantage and great success, when he was welcomed by every clergyman, and hailed by every school, gave rise to a similar course, but doubtless, less regular, as recognized by any ecclesiastical sanction, than the course pursued afterwards by Rowlands of Llangeitho, which eventually led to his ejection

[1] See Archdeacon Bather's "Hints on Catechisms," a most valuable little volume.

from the Church, an event which has ever since been much deplored, and even to this day not as lightly felt.

These schools, for twenty years after Mr Griffith Jones' death, were conducted under the superintendence and directions of Mrs Beavan herself, who, at her death, for their future management and support, bequeathed the munificent sum of £10,000, an act which has ever endeared her name to her native country, and which generations yet unborn will bless and praise. A legacy bequeathed with prudence, foresight, and benevolence, ascends higher than the praises of men, and touches a chord which vibrates in the Eternal Bosom. Such self-denying deeds, exercised in the spirit of faith amongst men, become memorials before God. Education, based on the principles recognized in Mrs Beavan's school, whilst intended for the lower and poorer classes of society, aims at man's highest culture. Griffith Jones was highly gifted as a preacher, and, since the days of the venerable vicar of Llandovery, had drawn larger crowds to attend his ministry than any of his contemporaries or his predecessors. He was no great orator, and never attempted to cultivate oratory as an art, though he never despised such subsidiary means, yet he never relied nor depended upon such extrinsic sources. He possessed higher eloquence than oratory, and spoke a language which all the arts of oratory can neither cultivate nor furnish. We can imitate to perfection the most lovely rose that ever budded, or the most delicious fruit that ever grew; but to impart to the wax the sweet fragrance of the rose, or endue the imitation with the delicious taste of the grape, is a thing unknown to art, and does not lie within the province of man. The highest gifts of art are nothing but imitations. Griffith Jones was real, and in earnest. He seldom employed any metaphors, and not frequently indulged in any similes, yet, withal, he handled the word of truth with uncommon success. He never left the point whence he started, but gradually unfolded it, enlarging upon it now and then, and continually adducing proofs to support his argument; and then, in masterly manner, he would sum up the whole discourse, illustrating the force of his evidence by appealing to particular instances, and furnishing particular examples. He was one of those who rightly divided the word of truth, and whilst handling the truth, he felt its force. The grand secret of his success was a deep-rooted conviction in his own soul. The fire which burnt on that altar which he had consecrated to God, consumed also every true sacrifice which had been brought to the temple. His manner was so impressive, his demeanour so solemn—indeed, his whole action bespoke a man earnestly and intensely engaged in those momentous matters of life and death.

> "He preached as if he would ne'er preach again,
> As dying man to dying men."

Mr Griffith Jones devoted the best energies of a useful life to the interest of his Church and the benefit of his nation. His valuable services, which were buried with him in the grave, had been highly appreciated by his contemporaries; and his writings, which survive him, are not less appreciated by his posterity. He worked hard, and wrote much. His "Platform of Christianity," being an explanation of the Thirty-nine Articles of the Church of England, has been much admired for its simplicity and orthodoxy, but it has never been adopted at any college as a standard text-book. A letter written by a clergyman, evincing the necessity of teaching the poor in Wales, only manifests the longing desire to effect their moral and spiritual improvement—a subject that had engaged his attention, and employed his head and hand nearly all his lifetime.

"The Christian Covenant, or Baptismal Vow," recognizes the great principles which the Christian Church has been teaching in all ages.

"His Exposition of the Church Catechism," in Welsh, needs no comment—it is quite a master-piece, which contains the essence of divinity, and illustrates, in a most practical and useful manner, the great truths of Christianity. "His Invitation to the Throne of Grace," and his "Guide to the Throne of Grace," contain much matter similar to an admirable little book which has met with extraordinary circulation, "Heaven our Home." His "Form of Prayers," for domestic and other purposes, has been much admired and much used. His "Free Counsel;" his "Encouragement to Praise God;" his "Letter on the Duty of Teaching the Unlearned;" and his "Collection of Vicar Prichard's Poems," all bear the touch of his pen, the diligence and sagacity of his hand and head, as well as the goodness of his heart. After a life of active service, diligently, but unostentatiously employed in his Master's service, this good and faithful servant was called to rest from his labours in 1761, being seventy-six years of age, and was buried at Llanddowrwr, a church which he had served for forty-five years, and where a monument, erected by Mrs Beavan, marks the place where his ashes rest in peace.

ROWLANDS' MEMOIR.

Daniel Rowlands, generally known as "Rowlands of Llangeitho," was born at a place called Pant-y-beudy, in the parish of Llancwnlle, Cardiganshire, in the year 1713. His father was the incumbent both of Llangeitho and Llancwnlle.

Not much is known of the family, but "the character of the father, though variously represented with respect to religion, appears to have been happily decided, at least in the latter part of his life. He then saw the necessity of true religion, both for himself and others. The state of his countrymen excited his compassion, and led him beyond that sphere of exertion which the rules of an establishment had prescribed. To what extent his itinerant labours were carried on, or with what success they were blessed, cannot now, perhaps, be ascertained; but in consequence of his endeavours to do good in this way, he is said to have suffered the loss of some preferment."[1] This may materially account for the origin of dissent, which, at least in Wales, did not spring out of doctrinal differences. It was the movement of a religious earnestness, chafing against the restraints imposed upon it, as was thought, by cold profession and worldly formalism. Whatever faults we may find in the first revolters against ecclesiastical discipline and rule, no one has ever doubted their religious earnestness, and simple conscientious devotion to religious truth, as taught in the standards and formularies of the Church. Many such are still to be found in the ranks of Nonconformists, so they cannot be drawn from thence by any display of activity and diligence which is not manifestly stimulated by the love of Christ our Saviour, and a desire for the salvation of souls. How long, or to what extent the hostility against the Church, which has of late years shown itself with so much bitterness, will be allowed to prevail, God only knows. But let us believe that it can never be overcome by the use of carnal weapons, and let us be on our guard against encouraging a carnal spirit.

Such sentiments form a basis, and furnish a key to actions, which appear to some irregular, but which others regard as the work of the

---

[1] Rowlands' "Memoir," by Rev. J. Owen.—p. 10.

Spirit. Upon this hypothesis we proceed to narrate the history of Rowlands' life. Of Rowlands' early career we are not furnished with any interesting particulars. He was educated at the public grammar school at Hereford, where he made rapid progress in learning, especially in the study of languages, and in consequence of his great proficiency, he was admitted as a candidate for holy orders before the usual age, and was ordained in London, by letters demissory, in 1733, when he was only twenty years old. He became now a curate to his brother John, who had been promoted to his father's livings, upon his father's death in 1731. Rowlands had also, not long after he was ordained, the charge of Ystradffin, Carmarthenshire, where he was highly esteemed by his parishioners, who "admired his ability as a preacher, but were chiefly attached to him because of the brilliancy of his wit, and the sweetness of his disposition.

A Mr Pugh, an earnest, simple, good man, was living at Blaenpenal, in the neighbourhood of Llangeitho, as a dissenting preacher, whose ministry met with great success. Whilst only a few attended the church at Llangeitho, crowds were seen wending their way to the little chapel at Blaenpenal. This induced Rowlands to attend Mr Pugh's ministry, and thereby learn the secret whereby his labours were crowned with so much success. When he found that the mode pursued at Blaenpenal was to alarm the careless, to arouse the sluggard, and to awaken the dead, he hastened back to Llangeitho, selecting such texts as were best calculated to produce the same effect, such as, " The wicked shall be turned into hell;" " These shall go away into everlasting fire," &c. From these he advanced such truths, with such force and power, as created a deep impression. Crowds were soon seen at the church, and the course which he pursued turned out a great success. At this time an event occurred which gave still greater stimulus to his energy, and moved the great depth of his fervour. The Rev. Griffith Jones, Llanddowrwr, the founder of the circulating schools in Wales, and an immensely popular preacher in the principality, was in the habit of preaching at different churches, whilst on his tour to visit his schools. In one of these journeys he was engaged to preach at Llanddewibrefi, where Rowlands, with many others, went to hear him. The sermon produced a powerful effect on his mind, which made him feel no strength in his body. He was much affected, and became mightily humbled. It is said that Rowlands stood in a bold attitude before the preacher, who, in the midst of his sermon, directed his eyes towards heaven, and implored a blessing upon that young man, that he might be humbled, and become as a little child.

On his returning home, he heard the people loudly expressing their approbation of the preacher, when one in the company exclaimed, " Say what you will of the sermon, I have reasons to thank God for the young minister of Llangeitho," at the same time advancing forward and tapping Rowlands on the shoulder in an encouraging manner. " Who knows," said Rowlands to himself, " but that God may still employ my humble service for His great glory." The Sunday games, sanctioned by Laud whilst Bishop of St David's, had produced many evil effects. These, which desecrated the churchyard, had become scenes of pitched battles, where oaths and curses were freely mingled with their blood and bruises. After the effect produced on Rowlands' mind on hearing Griffith Jones's sermon, he, with greater energy than ever, applied all his great talents against these evil practices, and often continued to preach till night, that, by the aid of nature and by the means of grace, an end might be put to such proceedings. Such irresistible power and divine grace accompanied his ministry, that the effect was most astonishing, and the result creating a great moral change. Not only were the churches filled, but the churchyards too. He thundered the law in such a terrible manner as created an impression, so awful and distressing, that many saw, as it were, the day of judgment before their eyes, and hell yawning beneath their feet.

The following circumstances may serve to convey an idea of the impression created by God's grace on men's minds at this time. A farmer's wife, living at a considerable distance, came on a visit to her sister at Llangeitho, and as a matter of course went on Sunday to hear the *mad* preacher. The effect produced on her mind she did not communicate to her sister, but, like Mary, pondered the truth she had heard, deeply in her heart; for her sister seemed surprised to find her again coming on the next Sunday to her house in order to attend at the same church. This she continued to do for a long time, until at length she prevailed upon Rowlands to go and preach in her own neighbourhood. In that neighbourhood, the country squire was a man of dissolute habits, and often, on the Lord's day, he was seen, with his tenants and dogs, engaged in the pursuits and pleasure of the chase. On the Sunday Rowlands was to preach, he went out earlier than usual in pursuit of his pleasures, that he might go afterwards to hear the preacher. From the field he went to church; he stood up in his seat, which was opposite the pulpit, and with an air of bold defiance, confronted the preacher's powers in a manner that dared the force of his truth. But Rowlands' weapons were not carnal. He dived into his subject with all the energies of his soul. He forgot man, and centred himself in the strength of God. He was awful and terrific. Claps of his thunder, one moment, created an awful dread, and the next minute, flashes of lightning penetrated their dark souls. The whole assembly stood mute, amazed, and confounded, and, behold, the strongholds of the great man had given way. The defiant eye was cast on the ground. Confusion of face struggled with his former pride. Fear seized his inward soul. He shook like a leaf. He quaked like a tottering old man. He sat in his corner, and wept like a child. When the service was over, the squire hastened to make confessions of his sin to the preacher, and the preacher was ready to administer the balm of consolation to his soul. A bond of union was thus cemented by mutual love, and friendship thus begun continued uninterrupted, nay, waxing stronger, through life, and ceased not in death; for love is not only a tie existing through things present, but a link in the communion of saints, which does not snap asunder in death. Either as long as Rowlands preached, or as long as the squire lived, the squire of Ystradffin never ceased to attend the ministry of Rowlands of

Llangeitho. So mighty through God are the weapons of our warfare to demolish the strongholds of Satan.

It appears that soon after these events Rowlands began his itinerant preaching, and the great success which attended the ministry of Griffith Jones, in a similar manner, and his own father on several occasions in his latter days, furnished examples which, to him, justified the conduct he pursued, and gave him great encouragement in the course he adopted. His bowels also yearned over the sad state of his country, and his soul longed to make known unto them the way of salvation. He who, as a boy, was foremost in every species of wickedness, the champion of their Sunday games, and the leader of their Sunday plots, had now put away his childish things, and assumed the leadership of a more worthy cause. With firm step, fixed eye, and undaunted courage, he resorted to these unhallowed meetings, and with a loud voice condemned their sinful proceedings. His eye flashed truth : every word told that he spoke his Master's message. The fire of heaven had touched his heart, and love for his Master's service, as fire descending upon the altar of his heart—a true burnt-offering—consumed his inner man. These Sabbath-breakers were convinced that God *owned* His servant. Wherever he went, he struck awe into their assemblies—some ran for their life—others trembled with fear—and all were alarmed and distressed.

This great change in Rowlands' life many call conversion. But would not the term conversion be more applicable to a person converted from heathenism and Judaism, to embrace the Christian religion? Would it not be more consistent to denote such a change in a person who had been baptized in the blessed name of God the Father, God the Son, and God the Holy Spirit, and brought up in the knowledge of the essentials of the Christian's creed, by repentance, renewal, or renovation? It is to be feared that religious differences often arise from attaching different meanings to words which convey the same religious import.

Rowlands' preaching had been hitherto, as we have observed, of a very terrifying character, fulminating the thunders of the law, its vengeance and curses, in such a teriffic manner, and with such a stamp of reality, as made many feel utterly overwhelmed with despair. At this time, the good old dissenting preacher, Mr Pugh, who had on several occasions returned Rowlands the compliment, and was a great admirer of Rowlands' preaching, now proffered Rowlands his advice, telling him "to preach the Gospel to the people, and apply the blood of Christ to their spiritual wounds, showing them the necessity of faith in the crucified Saviour." "I am afraid," said Rowlands, "that I have not that faith myself in its vigour and full exercise." "Preach on it," said Pugh, "till you find it in that way, no doubt it will come. If you go on preaching the law in this manner, you will kill half the people in the country, for you thunder out the curses of the law in such a teriffic manner that no one can stand before you." Pugh also gave him some judicious counsels touching his manner of preaching, which he much valued, though one habit he never discontinued. He used to stretch out his arm, clenching his fist except one finger, which, in his animated manner of preaching, many believed was pointed at them personally, like an arrow planting convictions in their souls—a personal message declaring solemnly to each, "Thou art the man." When Rowlands learned the great effect produced by his pointed finger, "I declare," said he "I will never discontinue that useful practice." Though Rowlands at this time had many trials to contend with, yet his aged counsellor never attempted to make him dissatisfied with his position in the Church, and bring such an eminent leader to head the ranks of dissent, but exhorted him to remain faithful at his post, and proceed in his duties as directed by Providence. It is supposed, though not certainly known, that about the year 1737 Rowlands and Howel Harris met each other,—the one in Cardiganshire, and the other in Breconshire, the latter a layman, the former a clergyman—unknown to each other, yet about the same time, originated and pursued a system which produced similar effects. Ahab regarded Elijah as the one who "troubled Israel." Rowlands and Harris were by many regarded as disturbing the peace. Yet nobody can deny but that they were instruments in the hands of God, whereby great changes were effected, and many souls saved. God owned the service of His servants, and made them a blessing to His people. They were not animated by any worldly motives, but sacrificed worldly interest. They courted no favour, and sought no reward. They lived to serve God, and worked to save souls.

Clywch hen delynor Pantycelyn.
"Dyma'r pryd daeth Harris fywiog
Yn arfogaeth fawr y nef
Megis taran annioddefol,
Yno i'w gyfarfod ef;
Dyma ddyddian Sylfaen gobaith
Dyddian gwewyr llym a phoen,
Wrth gael esgor ar ei meibion
Newydd wraig yr addfwyn Oen."

Whilst Rowlands and Harris were creating a new life in Wales, Wesley and Whitfield were spreading a new light in England.[1] The action seemed a simultaneous combustion. Did not the fire descend from the same source, at the same time, and for the same end? General corruption had spread over the country, general indifference characterized the nation, and however much writers of the present day ignore the fact,[2] our credibility rests on the unshaken testimony of that age. In 1736, Bishop Butler, in his preface to the "Analogy," corroborates our assertion. "It has come," says this good bishop, "I know not how, to be taken for granted by many persons, that Christianity is not so much as a subject for inquiry, but that it is now at length discovered to be fiction; and accordingly they treat it as if, in the present age, this were an agreed point among all people of discernment, and that nothing remained but to set it up as a principal subject for mirth and ridicule, by way of reprisals, for its having so long, as it were, interrupted the pleasures of the world." The united exertions of these cham-

[1] All historians, from Hume the infidel, and Lingard the Roman Catholic, down to Macaulay and Froude, acknowledge the change effected, and the good produced by the preaching of Wesley and Whitfield in England, yet Rowlands and Harris were in no degree less successful in Wales.

[2] See remarks by Eben Fardd, Cynddelw, and Ioan Emlyn, to Tudur's successful poem on Rowlands, Llangeitho, "Yr Eisteddfod."—Nov. 1, 1864.

pions of the truth were, doubtless under God's blessing, effectual in stemming this tide of corruption.[1] We do not know how many had joined Wesley[2] and Whitfield in their movement in England: we know that no less than ten clergymen had joined Rowlands and Harris in Wales.[3] They had no idea of causing any divisions in the Church, much less any secession from her communion. "The revival of religion in the Church was their avowed object from the first, and their professed object through life."[4]

Our history now brings us to that period in Rowlands' life which witnessed great changes in his manner of preaching. He now began to preach the Gospel in all its sublime excellences. His manner was moving, winning, and most captivating; and though he exhibited the dole-

---

[1] See Buck's "Theological Dictionary."—Vol. II.

[2] It is singular, that, on the misconception of the mild apologetic reply of Jesus, many amongst Papists and Protestants have really considered that to be careless of their dress is an act of piety. Whitfield takes care to write in his journals, "My apparel was mean—thought it unbecoming a penitent to have *powdered hair*. I wore *woollen gloves*, a *patched gown*, and *dirty shoes*." The description given by Macaulay of that singular character, George Fox, appears more fantastic still. It does not merely provoke a smile, but it is hard to suppress a hearty laugh.

[3] Harris's Letter to Whitfield, Oct. 15, 1742. Morgan's "Life of Harris."

[4] Owen's "Memoir of Rowlands."—Page 27.

ful state of the damned with such reality and life-like colours, that one might have supposed he had seen hell itself, and had been an eye-witness of all the dreadful consequences of sin in another world,[1] yet he enforced the truth with the most melting persuasions, entreating his hearers, with peculiar tenderness, as being himself most sensitively alive to the awful consequences, to shun the doomed abyss of sin and hell. The sublimity of that awfulness, which struck terror to every soul, was now so blended with that softness and tenderness of feeling which melted every heart. The awfulness of Mount Sinai seemed heightened by the lovingness of Mount Zion. On the one hand, God seemed invested in all the majesty of His law. On the other, God in His Son, clothed in all the sweetness of His love. An immense concourse stood amazed: tears ran down their faces, and groans rose up from their hearts. The thoughtless stood aghast, as on the brink of despair; the proud seemed cast down, nigh to hell: and all wept, most wept for their sins,—a few wept for joy. At this time began that revivalism in Wales which lasted fifty years. The first im-

---

[1] See Cary's Translation of Dante, whose descriptions of hell seem *almost real and life-like*. Macaulay instances Cary's translation as one of those rare occurrences where the translation is superior to the original.

pulse took place in a remarkable manner. When Rowlands was reading the Litany at church on Sunday morning, his whole soul seemed to be deeply engaged in prayer, and his whole mind wrapped up in divine contemplation, and upon a sudden he felt an overwhelming force, as of a mighty rushing power, filling every faculty of his soul, which breathed into his prayer the breath of life, and stamped every accent with touching reality, as he gave utterance to the following words : " By thine agony and bloody sweat, by thy cross and passion, by thy precious death and burial, by thy glorious resurrection and ascension, and by the coming of the Holy Ghost." His whole soul seemed entranced in heavenly raptures, his vigorous frame shook, as tottering to the ground. The shock instantly, like lightning, sent a thrill through the crowd, and many in the congregation fell on their knees. The whole church presented an affecting scene. In a similar manner, as the congregation was deeply affected by Rowlands' preaching, the country was aroused by the effects produced upon the hearers. These were no ephemeral flashes, which spread death and desolation wherever they swept their course, and sped their way. The impression was permanent. It continued to grow during Rowlands' ministry, and produced effects which lasted for generations, and continued to our own day. Revivals have since occurred in this country,[1] in Ireland, and in America, but in most instances they were produced by external force, the effect transient, and the result often unfavourable and unsatisfactory. On the contrary, the revival originated by Rowlands was the result of spiritual impressions and religious convictions: the truth which he so deeply felt inwardly in his own soul, produced an effect which he could not fail to express outwardly in his preaching. It touched the hearts of his hearers, and impregnated the whole principality of Wales. The domestic hearth became a consecrated altar, whence the morning and evening sacrifice of prayer have never ceased to ascend. By the firesides songs of praises were heard, and by death-beds happy scenes were witnessed. The light of divine truth, which at this time shone on Rowlands' mind, continued to shine with increasing brightness during his long career: it was burning in

---

[1] In a shilling volume published by Routledge, "Religion in Wales," the author, speaking of revivals, writes in a note as follows:—"The writer was lately on a visit in Cardiganshire; he learned there is now a revival in a part of that country. It commenced in a church not far from Aberystwyth." The church here referred to was Llanrhystyd, and the revival originated under the powerful preaching of Rev. W. Hughes, now Rector of Caerwys, Flintshire.

his vessel when he was summoned to meet the Bridegroom; it guided him through life, and led him to glory.

Rowlands, at an early age, occupied very important positions. In his own eyes he was less than the least of his brethren, but in their eyes he was regarded as by far the greatest, and their leader. At the age of twenty-seven he was the chairman of the great association which has been attended by thousands, and which flourishes even in our own days. Rowlands was much assisted in these movements by two well known names in the principality, one for his poetry, the other for his commentary. As much as John Keble was considered eminently the poet of the Christian life of the nineteenth century in England, so we may truly say of Williams, Pantycelyn,[1] that he was the Christian poet of the eighteenth century in Wales. Keble might soar higher, or dive deeper, but he did not sing sweeter, nor touched the heart with a livelier strain. And we venture to say that as long as Keble's poetry will excite the admiration of English hearts, the mountains of Wales will

---

[1] Sir Roundell Palmer, in his most interesting lecture on Hymnody, alludes to William Williams, Pantycelyn, as being the author of some of our sweetest hymns; and whoever consults his choice collections of hymns will find William Williams' name embalmed in that delightful volume.

resound with the strains of Williams' hymns. The sweet melody of divine truth wherewith William Williams' poetry affected the heart, has, nevertheless, never been more highly esteemed than P. Williams' commentary, which has been so instrumental in enlightening the understanding. These men, who were as ready to lay down their lives for the truth as to give up their livings as regards worldly interest, were of immense assistance to Rowlands. They were to him as Aaron was to Moses—men of great conversational powers. Acquainted with every station in life, they could speak to every member in the Church, in a manner suitable to each, and in a manner edifying to all.

Rowlands' chequered career cannot be more lively represented than by imagining a clergyman's son brought up in the best school of his time, and serving his brother's church as a curate, at £10 per annum. When Goldsmith, at a later date, describes a country clergyman " passing rich upon £40 a year," we cease to wonder how another did not cease to exist upon £10. This generous pittance of a brother, in a twofold nature—by profession and blood—our feelings of resentment cannot spurn with too much indignation, but we grieve at heart to find an aged father, who had bravely fought the battle of truth, driven by persecution, and compelled by circumstances, to be his own son's curate, and finally to be ejected out of that Church wherein he had been born, and in which he had been brought up, and which he had for twenty-eight years served with unfeigned zeal, and which he loved with sincere affection. The ejectment occurred in 1763. The bishop's mandate was handed him immediately after reading the service at Llanddewibrefi. Great consternation seized the congregation, and Rowlands, not unlike Zacharias, who had been struck dumb in the temple, was so overwhelmed with astonishment and distress that he could hardly speak to the people. The punishment inflicted upon Zacharias was caused by his incredulity, the deprivation inflicted on Rowlands was the result of his faithfulness. The Church of England was thus deprived of the services of one of her most devoted and faithful sons, whom the Church of Rome would have hailed with joy as a man of true missionary spirit. The course which was then so *severely* condemned by the Bishop of St David's, is now pursued under the direction and sanction of the present Bishop of Llandaff. It is true, the bishop remonstrated with his conduct in traversing beyond the boundaries of his own parish, but he believed it his duty to " obey God rather than man," and declared he had no other object in view than the glory of

God, the salvation of souls, and the good of the Church. Dr Burgess, who next succeeded to the see of St David's, regretted this act of his predecessor, as the greatest mistake he had ever committed in his life. A chapel was now built for him at Llangeitho; and from that time until the day of his death, it is emphatically said, that on Sacrament Sundays no less than three or four thousand people attended his ministry. It is within the memory of scores now living, to have conversed with many who had been eye-witnesses of the scene, and partakers of its blessings. Hundreds were seen commencing their journey on Saturday night; and scores travelled no less than twenty miles, not a few forty, and some sixty miles. These crowds were no inapt antitypes of the tribes of Israel, who, at stated periods, resorted to Jerusalem to worship God. That Rowlands became the founder of a new sect, cannot be denied; that he dearly and sincerely loved the Church, admits of no doubt. He used the services of the Church in his chapel; he exhorted his son, on his dying bed, though he might be exposed to greater persecution than himself, never to leave the Church, nor to secede from her communion; he could discern the signs of the times; he anticipated great changes, and his prophecy has, in a great measure, been fulfilled. That he retained these strong feelings of affection for the Church is honourably borne out by the testimony of a Nonconformist of our own time.[1] We must bear in mind that Rowlands did not leave the Church of his own accord, but was *driven* therefrom, much against his will. The apostle, in allusion to the office of the Christian ministry, teaches us that no one should take upon him this office except he that is called, as Aaron was, yet we cannot close our eyes to the fact, that Rowlands was instrumental to the introduction of the lay element to discharge the sacred functions of the priesthood. The members of the Church may complain that they follow not them, nevertheless the Great Head of the Church may see them as working with Him. Many deem themselves as *His* servants, whose service He will never own. On the other hand, many rush into the sacred office with more self-confidence than authority, and with more zeal than knowledge—the strange fire of Korah, Dathan and Abiram. They who establish their authority by an inward testimony, should adduce proofs by an outward evidence; and they who claim an authority by an external rite, should establish their mission by preaching sound doctrine, and leading a holy life.

The Roman Catholic Church exalts the rite

[1] *Vide* Owen Jones's Preface to "Rowlands' Sermons." Printed at Dowlais, 1862.

of ordination into a sacrament, and claims it as a badge of unbroken succession, and essential to her priesthood. Yet of what value can be its boasted succession, when she overlays some portions of Scripture with traditions, and removes other portions for her own convenience. The Apostle St Paul seems to demolish the claims of such pretensions, when he says, "though we (apostles), or an angel from heaven, preach any other gospel unto you than that which we have preached unto you, let him be accursed." If this, then, be said of an apostle, surely it might be said of an apostle's successor. And if it is said of an angel, surely it might be said of a man. The testimony of an angel is to be tried by the Scripture, and the preaching of an apostle is to be tested by the Word of God. The rule and standard of our faith can neither be the pretensions of man, nor the claims of the Church, but the lively oracles of the living God. Ordination is now a rite generally practised amongst all denominations of Christians, and seems to be a principle which pervades all religions, whether Paganism or Christianity, and whether of ancient or modern times. In the patriarchal ages, heads of families acted as priests. Under the Mosaic dispensation, a particular tribe was set apart for the service of the temple by God himself. Our Saviour selected from amongst

His followers twelve apostles, also seventy disciples. After His resurrection, He furnished His apostles with the well-known commission, "Go ye," &c. After His ascension, St Peter stated the necessity of appointing an apostle in the room of Judas Iscariot, when the lot fell upon Matthias. It appears, from a variety of authorities, that the ordination of priests and deacons was practised in the early ages of Christianity; and even Jerome, who was no friend of Episcopacy, acknowledges ordination to be a bishop's office. "What does a bishop do," saith he, "except ordaining, which a presbyter cannot do."

Ordination, if not always essentially necessary, seems at least always desirable; whereas succession represents a chain of broken links, for which history supplies no positive evidence, and Scripture prescribes no particular form, save the imposition of hands. This digression in Rowlands' history appears almost necessary, showing how the rite of ordination is differently regarded by different people, and how Rowlands departed from a form of ordination which he had himself received. He who made the one Book his sole study, especially the New Testament portion, was more absorbed in the inward truths of the Gospel than the outward forms of Christianity; and whilst he became more indifferent as to the externals of religion, his soul clung more intensely than ever to the great essentials of salvation. "Believe in the Lord Jesus Christ," was his first starting point, and his last goal.

Our next step will be to treat of Rowlands' preaching. This was not less remarkable than effective, and not only amongst all the preachers of Wales he holds the pre-eminence, but is equal to, and as great as, any that appeared on the platform of Christendom since the days of the apostles. It may not be uninteresting to furnish a specimen of his preaching, and manner of addressing in the open air the immense crowds that flocked to hear him whilst visiting different parts of the principality. Once, whilst preaching on the following verse from the prophecy of Jeremiah, "And their nobles shall be of themselves, and their governors shall proceed from the midst of them, and I will cause him to draw near, and he shall approach unto me, for who is this that engaged his heart to approach unto me, saith the Lord."[1] He dwelt on the excellences of the "Prince of Peace" with such sublimity and magnificence that the whole scene represented a real sight of human nature having reached perfection in all its conceivable grandeur, putting on her eternal robe of divine glory.

[1] See an excellent Sermon on that subject by the great Robert Hall.—Vol. v.

"He personified Law and Justice in the most striking and feeling manner, both demanding the infinite punishment the Blessed Surety had engaged, in the everlasting covenant, in order to effect the redemption of sinful men. He expressed himself in the following moving manner as he was setting forth those agonizing truths:

"'Be it known unto thee,' said Justice, 'that though thou comest to thine own as their Saviour, yet thou must dwell with the cattle at thy first entrance: a manger shall be thy cradle, and rags shall be thy clothing.' However, the Surety did not shrink in the least at this, but answered, 'I am perfectly willing, for the sake of my people, to undergo even that treatment.' 'If thou goest into a world that is under a curse,' said the Law, 'thou shalt not have a place to lay thy head upon, yea, thou shalt be the object of the utmost wrath, malice, and envy of creatures that are supported by thee every moment.' He answers, 'Oh, my pure Law, I am willing to endure all that also.' 'But,' said Justice, 'thou must sweat great drops of blood on a cold night in a garden, and thy enemies shall spit in thy face, they shall scourge thy sacred back, and crown thy blessed head with thorns: yea, thy own disciples, even after seeing thy great miracles, and hearing thy heavenly doctrine, will forsake thee when in the greatest difficulty and distress: yea, one of them will even sell thee, and another will deny thee, cursing and swearing most fiercely he does not know thee.' 'Yet,' exclaims the Surety, 'notwithstanding all this unkindness and cruelty, I will not withdraw from my engagement—no, not on any account: repentance shall be hid from mine eyes.' Law and Justice now testify together, saying, 'O thou, the glorious object of adoration and praise of all the angelic heavenly host, and the infinite delight of God the Father, if thou wilt actually enter upon this suretyship, all the powers of hell will be in array against thee to assail thee; and even the unmixed wrath of Heaven will be poured out upon thy soul and body upon the cross! yea, to tell thee all, the last drop of thy heart's blood shall be shed!— the unspeakable agony of all this thou must endure.' And now, my dear hearers," said Rowlands, "who can—without astonishment think of this gracious Surety engaging, in the face of all these dreadful storms, to undertake the mighty work—think that, in the full view of all these most alarming and painful sufferings, He should exclaim, *I am perfectly willing!*"

Another still more striking instance has been related of Rowlands' preaching powers. In several places which he visited he was subjected to incredible annoyance and malicious persecutions; but in one place a most diabolical plot had been conceived and planned. It was another gunpowder plot. The spot where he would be preaching was well known beforehand, and underneath that very place was deposited a quantity of powder, and the whole scheme had been so arranged, without incurring the danger which the infatuated Guy Fawkes, in his blind zeal, had sworn to risk and was ready to sacrifice. However, the discovery of some straw excited suspicions, and frustrated their hellish design; and whilst declaiming against the vices of the people, and representing to them, one by one, the calamities God would send upon them on this account, he added, in conclusion, in a stentorian voice, and with an authority which rushed with irresistible force, and " God will for ever abandon you." Then he resumed in a low, wailing, and weeping tone, extremely penetrating, touching, and pitiable, moving all to tears, when in a supplicatory attitude, he exclaimed, " If thou dost abandon us, merciful God, what will become of us!"

The testimony of Charles of Bala, the great originator of the Bible Society, whose field of operation at the present day extends nearly over the habitable globe, as to the effect produced on him cannot be omitted. He says, "I went to hear Mr Rowlands preach. The text was Heb. iv.

15, 'For we have not an high priest which cannot be touched with the feeling of our infirmities, but was in all points tempted like as we are, yet without sin.' A day," saith he, "much to be remembered by me as long as I live. Ever since that day I have lived in a new heaven and a new earth. A change which a blind man who receives his sight experiences, does not exceed the change which at that time I experienced in my mind. It was then I was first convinced of the sin of unbelief, or entertaining narrow, contracted, and hard thoughts of the Almighty. I had such a view of Christ as our high priest, of His love, compassion, power, and all sufficiency, as filled my soul with astonishment, with joy unspeakable and full of glory. My mind was overwhelmed and overpowered with amazement. The glorious scenes then opened to my eyes will abundantly satisfy my soul *millions* of years hence in the contemplations of them. I had some ideas of gospel truths before floating in my mind, but they never powerfully, and with divine energy, entered my heart until now."

Rowlands, like Robert Hall in his sermon upon the Signs of the Times, deemed any revival in the Church as the brightest prospect, rejoiced with exceeding joy whenever any signs of a new life sprung up in the bosom of the old

Paradise, and when a young clergyman of great promise was cut down in the midst of his useful career, "Alas!" cried he, "my right hand is cut off."

Rowlands' peculiar domain was preaching, and in proof of our assertion we adduce our evidence. One eminent man, writing in his diary on a certain day, many years after he had heard Rowlands preach, remarks, "Every return of this blessed day is refreshing to my soul. The remembrance of the mercies which I received can *never* be forgotten. That aged herald of the King of Glory, D. Rowlands, will be an *eternal* glory to Wales. I can seldom speak of him in *moderate* terms. I love him dearly as my father in Christ. I hope to see him once more before he takes his flight." An aged clergyman, occupying a well known position, and having heard the most eminent preachers in England and Wales, declared he had only heard *one* Rowlands, implying, that he vastly surpassed all others. Another saith of him, "His zeal, animation, and fervour surpassed all description. I never in my life saw anything so expressive, it reminded me almost of an angel." Those striking words, "He maketh his ministers a flame of fire," seem verified in him. Some describe his words like darts, reaching here, and there, and everywhere, yet effectual in every instance. One clergyman, who had known him for a number of years, thus describes him: — " For forty years he has been a zealous and indefatigable labourer in the Lord's vineyard, and, notwithstanding his great age, he is as active as ever. Unembarassed with worldly cares, and almost unconnected with the world, he lives above it, and is a striking emblem of primitive simplicity. Wholly devoted to his Master's work, and treading in his Master's steps, he goes about doing good. The number of his communicants on Sacrament Sundays is seldom less than two thousand—sometimes more than four thousand. He speaks from the heart, and draws his treasures from the sacred oracles, rousing his hearers to a sense of their danger by the thunders of the law and the lightning of Sinai. His soul being deeply impressed with the truth of God's Word, he preached thé glad tidings with all the fervour, affection, and reality, as one who knew by the experience of an inward testimony their inestimable value." In the very midst of a torrent of eloquence, whilst dwelling on the inestimable riches of Christ, he would turn his eye heavenward, and in a most rapturous and elevated strain, he would invoke God's Spirit to breathe into their souls the breath of life, that they might come to their Saviour and partake of His riches. He illustrated his subject by Scriptural references, and from some object, either well known or visible, he employed such apt similes as must be intelligible to the dullest mind. He thus opened their understandings as well as their hearts, and through the instrumentality of Divine grace, which accompanied his preaching, thousands were brought from darkness to light, and from the power of Satan to God.

His bursts of eloquence resembled the gradual swellings of the sea, when its bosom begins to be agitated by winds, the forerunners of hurricanes. He commenced calmly, but as he advanced, his manner became more animated, and his matter more interesting—like wave upon wave, swelling and increasing, running with great force, and carrying away everything in their awful currents, and in tempestuous fury meet, clash, and break. Between their yawning gulfs you see the deeps of the ocean, groaning and murmuring as if the elements of heaven were working out its final doom. Again, marching in mountainous torrents on the ocean's deep, as if to outrival the clouds which sweep under heaven. Thus Rowlands carried the minds, hearts, and feelings of his audience with him, with such gentleness and sweetness that was captivating and enchanting; then on a sudden he would plunge them into all the horrors of despair, and with a power and force quite irresistible, led them to behold the unutterable anguish of the lost, and made them feel the doleful miseries of the damned. What Dante has so awfully described in the language of poetry, Rowlands preached with all the conviction of truth: then groans and moanings and lamentations echoed their saddened and doleful notes through a thousand hearts, touched by the spirit of conviction, exclaiming, What shall we do to be saved,—and now, being excited to the highest pitch that religious emotion can burn in a mortal soul, he seemed to scale the pinnacles of glory, and display to their wondering eyes God's amazing love, and from the inexhaustible riches of eternity, bringing out to each, as if to the prodigal son, the best robe of Christ's righteousness. Then their joy in believing. Their groanings ceased, and their hosannahs and hallelujahs began. When his voice had reached its climax, it went forth like the bursting of a clap of thunder, and he poured forth his mighty message, with such extraordinary torrents of eloquence as overwhelmed and overpowered his audience. His attitude, his voice, his gesture, his striking manner, his noble and impressive mien, and, above all, his strong religious impression, and his deep religious conviction, his burning zeal, and his intense love, were rare endowments, and such uncommon gifts, as qualified this great and good man, in an eminent degree, to be the ambassador of the most high God. It was once asked a gentleman who had heard Rowlands preach, in what consisted the peculiarity of Rowlands' preaching. "I'll tell you," said he, "*depth* and *fervour*."

Like Jacob wrestling with the angel for a blessing, Rowlands had often been seen, especially on Sunday mornings, labouring under a feeling of intense mental agony—actually wrestling in prayer—importunately urging his suit before the throne of grace, and had been heard to declare aloud, like Moses of old, "If thy presence go not with me, carry me not up hence."

Rowlands in his private life was as gentle as a lamb. He received all friends with an open hand and an open heart. For kindness, tenderness, and sympathy, humanity could not furnish a nobler specimen of her handiwork. Yet, withal, he was as bold as a lion, intrepid as a martyr, and fearless as an angel. Like his great Master, who, in compassion, said, "Go, and sin no more," Rowlands deeply sympathized with all the miseries and weakness of human nature. Yet, with all the energy of his amazing powers, he denounced all hypocrisy, deceit, and sin, in a language as fearless as characterized the conduct of the Pharisees, "Ye serpents, ye generation of vipers, how can ye escape the damnation of hell."

A working man furnished an original idea, when he was asked what he thought of Whitfield's preaching, " he preaches like a lion," said he. Still, when Whitfield's voice was most enchanting, his matter was less interesting; whereas Rowlands, when his voice had reached its climax, launched forth the pith of his message, like a thunderstorm in the height of its sublime solitude and awful grandeur, shoots down hailstones amongst its awful cataracts.

ROWLANDS' SUCCESS.

Independent of any testimony—of the crowds that attended his ministry, of the number of miles they travelled, or the number of years they attended—nothing known is more beautifully illustrated than the history of any other preacher, by the following touching story:—On coming over a mountain, having reached its summit, when an extensive landscape and rich scenery opened to his view, and beginning to descend, he seemed unusually downcast—large tears rolled down his face, and his spirit seemed overwhelmed with grief. His friend asked him the cause of such emotions :—" Alas!" said he,

"I see many chimneys emitting smoke, but I see not a single hearth whence the morning incense of prayer has ascended up unto God." In coming over the same place many years after, he exclaimed, with a peculiar accent of unmistakeable joy:—"I see a number of houses scattered here and there before me, but not a single habitation where an altar has not been erected this morning unto the Lord of Hosts."

This famous herald of the everlasting Gospel, having run his course and kept the faith, was summoned hence to receive his reward—that crown of glory laid up for all who love the appearance of their Master's second advent. Having borne much fruit, he was ripe for the great harvest; having been a blessing to thousands, he was now blessed in his own soul; and having been faithful in his Master's service, he was now ushered in into his Master's joy. At the advanced age of seventy-seven years, October 16, 1790, he commended his spirit into the hands of Him who gave it.

"Blessed are the dead who die in the Lord."

Resurgam.

SERMON I.[1]

"Glad tidings of great joy."—MATTH. ii. 8, 9.

"AND he sent them to Bethlehem, and said, go and search diligently for the young child; and when you have found him, bring me word again, that I may come and worship him also. When they had heard the king, they departed; and lo! the star which they saw in the East went before them, till it came and stood over where the young child was."

When the Saviour of men was born into the world, the glad tidings of His birth were first announced to poor shepherds, "abiding in the field, and keeping watch over their flock by night." This is not the manner of men. They

---

[1] These sermons are said to have been originally and principally translated into English by the Rector of Escourt, whereas Escourt, as a *parish*, is a name unknown. For this information I am indebted to the learned T. James, F.S.A., F.G.H.S. (Llallawg), the incumbent of Netherthong, Huddersfield.

generally bestow their best things upon the greatest among them—upon kings and princes of the earth. They give poor things to the poor—such things as would not be acceptable to others. But Jesus Christ, the Pearl of great price—"the righteousness which looked down from heaven, and the truth which sprang from the earth," was first made known to men of low estate, whereby we are taught that no condition, however humble, poor, and low, is beneath God's notice, or is excluded, on that account, from sharing in the blessings of Christ. This, which subdues the pride of the high and lofty, teaches us that God communicates His grace to the humble and low. Yet, lest men of low estate should establish an exclusive right to Him, He was made manifest to the wise men from the East, whose treasures certainly proved them to be very rich, thus giving a full evidence of His readiness to save all ranks, and omit no degrees amongst the human race. He is the "tree that was in the midst of the garden"—the centre of grace which diffuses its influences everywhere around. As the tree of life, whose leaves were for the healing of the nations, is said to be "in the midst of the street," so is Jesus in the midst of His Church, communicating His grace to all, the poor as well as the rich, that all may become partakers of a divine nature. This should make all unite together in one common brotherhood, for neither the one nor the other can be saved, but through the merits of Jesus Christ. The very offering which the poor were enjoined to offer by the law of Moses, "a pair of turtle doves or two young pigeons"—which was the sacrifice of the Virgin Mary and her espoused husband when the Child Jesus was presented in the temple—amply proves their poverty. Yet it pleased the Prince of Glory to assume this form of poverty, that, through His poverty, many might be made rich. Let not the rich despise the poor, for He who was once contemptuously styled the carpenter's son, shall ere long be their eternal judge, and will take from them every talent not employed in his service. Let them remember that money can never redeem a single soul, or procure the least favour from an offended God. Our blessed Saviour has done more for us, by His poverty, than a thousand worlds can do for us by their treasures. "He has washed us from our sins in His own blood," and "made us kings and priests unto God."

Having before alluded to the wise men from the East, let us remember that the narrative is more immediately connected with them, and on this occasion more immediately interesting to us. The shepherds were Jews; the wise men were Gentiles. These were early intimations, that the prophecies foretold—*that "all the nations of the earth be blessed"*—would soon be realized, that "unto Him should the gathering of the people be," and that God should enlarge Japheth, and dwell in the tents of Shem. The delivering of the law on Mount Sinai, in Arabia, a Gentile land; the building of the temple on the threshing floor of Araunah, a Gentile ground, and the chief superintendence of the erection entrusted to Hiram, a Gentile by birth;—all very clearly show that the salvation which was originally confined to the Jews, should become also the inheritance of the Gentiles. These wise men were not only Gentiles, but doubtless men who feared God. The great distance did not debar them from undertaking the journey, nor did their great wealth render them careless about the salvation of their souls. This should instruct us that the wise and opulent have as much need of Jesus Christ as the ignorant and indigent. High and low must equally come to Him for salvation, for "there is no other name given amongst men whereby they can be saved." Princes, as well as their subjects, must go in through the same gate, or both perish without. The poor shepherds from the field, and the wise men from the East, came to pay their homage to Him who is the

Prince of Peace and the friend of sinners. Whatever be your condition—whether rich or poor, learned or unlearned—go, and search diligently for Him—lay hold on His righteousness and strength, and be ye saved through His mediation and merits. Here rich and poor meet together; both must have recourse to the same sacrifice. Under the law it was said, "the rich shall not give more, and the poor shall not give less, than half a shekel, when they give an offering to the Lord to make an atonement for their souls." There were other offerings in which the rich were required to give more than the poor, but in this—their daily offering—the amount was the same; the atoning sacrifice admitted neither increase nor decrease. This sacrifice was always the same, and to all persons it made no difference, a type—of Him who was the salvation of all men. "The same yesterday, to-day, and for ever."

I shall now consider whence the wise men came; where they came to; the end of their coming; the zeal and diligence in surmounting all difficulties; and the success wherewith it pleased God to crown their persevering researches; also the season of their coming. And may the Holy Spirit impress the truth of Christ coming upon our hearts, and be a guide to our souls, to lead us to our Saviour!

1. Whence the wise men came? They came from the East, a far distant country, and a journey not easy to undertake, but their coming was in accordance to the prophecies, which had foretold "that the Gentiles should come to His light, and kings to the brightness of His rising." God also himself had declared, "that many should come from the east, and from the west, and should sit down with Abraham, Isaac, and Jacob," and that the Gospel was to be preached to them who were afar off, as well as to those who were nigh. Gentiles, as well as Jews, were to be gathered into one fold, under one shepherd; and, behold, the gathering begins, for bringing us nigh who were once afar off, for admitting us who were aliens to the commonwealth of Israel into a share of their privileges, and for making us who had no hope and without God in the world, partakers of the rich blessings of the Gospel,—for all these we should give Him eternal praise. All now may come unto Him, that they may receive forgiveness of sin through faith in His name.

The wise men coming from a far country should teach us to spare no pains to seek Jesus, that we may be also found in Him. Though we should spend and be spent, though obstacles be in the way, and weariness in our journey, yet, if we can but find Jesus, and lay hold on

Him for our eternal life, our labour shall never be in vain. Every toil in the pursuit, and every effort in our search, if haply Christ be formed in our hearts, shall receive its due reward. Take heed lest the queen of the south should rise in judgment with this generation, and condemn them, because there is greater than Solomon here. Solomon was the wisest of men, but here is the Wisdom of God. Many who mind no distance, and regard no weather, to seek provision for the body, make no effort, and stir not a step, to seek salvation for their souls. They seek the bread that perisheth, but disregard the bread of life. It is sad to consider that these wise men—heathens in a distant country—should travel so many miles to seek Him who was born King of the Jews; whilst you, who call yourselves Christians, will not move or stir to seek the Saviour of your souls, who is the King of Glory. We show forth the Lord Jesus, not as the wise men, lying in a manger, bleeding in the garden, or dying on the cross, but sitting in unclouded majesty on His lofty throne in glory. May God remove every veil from off your heart, that you may see Him as He is,—more excellent than His angels, who excel in might.

2. We consider the place where the wise men came to. They came to Jerusalem, not by the

direction of the star, but by the guidance of their own reasoning. They naturally supposed that He who was to be born King of the Jews would be best known in their chief city, Jerusalem. But here they found Him not. They had been guided by the light of nature, when they should have been led by the light of the Spirit. Reason is a great and noble gift; it achieves great ends, and does that which is right, but it will never come to seek Jesus except drawn by the grace of God. "No man," saith our blessed Saviour, "can come unto me, except the Father who hath sent me, draw him." So long as the wise men followed the star, they steered their course aright. When they listened to the voice of reason, they lost the light of heaven. If the blind lead the blind, both shall fall into the ditch. We are blind by nature. Christ hath set up His Spirit to be our guide: may His light guide you through life, and at last bring you to your Saviour's presence, at whose right hand there are joys for evermore.

3. Our next inquiry is, What end the wise men had in view? Their object was to seek Jesus, and see Him. The wish was natural. He is the desire of all nations. Of old the same feelings have been expressed. Abraham did earnestly desire to see His day. "If I have," said Moses, "found grace in thy sight, show me, I

beseech thee, thy glory. We cannot see God and live." This is true, as He is God: but we may look upon the face of the Anointed of the Father and live—yea, live for ever. God sent forth His Son in the likeness of human flesh, and in Him our most earnest desire of seeing God may be fully realized. He is the express image of His person. "God said, Let us make man in our image"—that is, in the same image as He should afterwards appear in human form: and as He once made clay and applied it to the eyes of the blind man that He might see, even so He assumed human form, made of the dust of the ground, that He might be seen. Once to see Him, it is enough. Our souls are satisfied. We long to look upon no other object. "Lord, now lettest thou thy servant to depart in peace, for mine eyes have seen thy salvation." Let the worldly seek their gain; the covetous their wealth; and the libertine his pleasure; but seek ye Christ in your soul by faith. It was delightful to hear the angel say, "I know that ye seek Jesus." He seeks you. "The Son of Man is come to seek and to save that which was lost." Seek ye Him. As pants the hart for the cooling streams, so let your souls pant for the living God. "It pleased the Father that in Him should all fulness dwell." Seek ye Him, that ye may receive of His fulness, and grace for grace. No efforts would be spared to go and see an estate left us by another, — so " run that ye may obtain." He is the great prize of your salvation; rest not until you gain possession of your inheritance.

See the efforts which the wise men made. They came to Jerusalem, but they were disappointed. Their efforts met with no success. The priests of the temple and scribes of the law could furnish no information. The council of the Sanhedrim, and their glorious city—" the joy of the whole earth"—could form no attraction when Jesus was not to be found. Where He was not, they could not remain. This teaches us, that neither the indifference of the learned, nor carelessness of our superiors, should ever furnish an excuse for our negligence. Diligent in our duties, striving in our efforts. " our eyes" should never cease to "wait upon the Lord our God." Not for a day, nor for any particular time, but until He should have mercy upon us." " Though it tarry, wait for it; because it will surely come, it will not tarry," for " in due season we shall reap, if we faint not." The example of the wise men leaving Jerusalem should teach us to bid adieu to every place where the favour of God is not to be found, and where the things of God are not known. As they withdrew themselves from the celebrated city of Jerusalem, when they could not find Jesus there, so should each of us, whatever may be our condition in life, withdraw from the tents of the ungodly and the seats of the wicked, however inviting their appearance, or alluring their temptations. Rest not in your duties, nor place any confidence in your performances. Go on to seek the Lord until He is formed in your souls, and with a single eye look to Jesus as your hope of glory. Seek Him in His temples here below, that you may dwell with Him for ever in His tabernacle above.

Mark the success wherewith the Lord was pleased to crown the efforts of the wise men. Though they had received no instructions at Jerusalem touching the object of their mission, yet they had not gone far, "when, lo! the star which they saw in the east went before them, and stood over where the young Child was." Here we are encouraged to put ourselves entirely under the guidance of God's Spirit—to watch His motions, and quench not His strivings. The Lord will always accomplish that which He hath begun. Wherever He is the author of our faith, He is also the finisher. As we advance in the divine life, He unfolds the mystery of His grace. The stream may be small at its source, but it swells as it flows. Fresh springs flow in as we journey on. "To him who hath shall be given, and he shall have more abundance." God is ready to bless the efforts of His people, and quicken into life the work which the Spirit had begun in the soul.

4. We hasten now, in the last place, to make a few remarks on *the time* in which the wise men came. It was when Herod was king. This reminds us that Christ's kingdom was not of this world. He aspired not to Herod's throne, and though truly a king, was not of Herod's blood. Their inquiry was, "Where is he that is born King of the Jews;" and when He was asked, "Art thou a king?" His answer was, "To this end was I born, and for this cause came I into the world." "His kingdom is not of this world." Not a temporal, but a spiritual kingdom. This teaches us to moderate our wishes after earthly things—not to "receive honour one of another, but to covet that honour which cometh from God only." It should be our aim, not to be great in this world, but useful in our generation—not to be distinguished by wealth and splendour, but by meekness and lowliness of heart. Lazarus, covered with sores, was far dearer in the sight of God than the rich man in his power and glory. The hungry He fills with good things, the rich He sends empty away; the mighty He takes down from their seat, the humble He exalts many degrees.

It seems in accordance with God's will that He should not appear in His power, in His goodness, or in His might, until things have reached some extremity. He would not go to Bethany till " Lazarus had been dead four days." He would not go to His disciples, toiling all night, in danger, in the midst of the sea, until the fourth watch; so it was not His time to come into the world until the sceptre had departed from Judah, and matters reduced to great distress. He was to be the brother born for adversity. When the wine was all spent, He magnifies the power of His might. When we have a father or a mother to provide for us, He often passes by, but " when father and mother forsake us, the Lord will take us up." He is the Father of the fatherless, and God of all mercy. He loves His people at all times, but peculiarly manifests that love in the hour of distress. We will now conclude by the following remarks. Behold God's goodness in directing His people. He sent an angel to preach the Gospel to the shepherds, and directed a star to guide the wise men to Jesus. Blessed be His name. His Word is not only a star to guide our path, but a lamp to guide our feet. Faithful ministers direct our course, and God's Holy Spirit leads us to all truth. May we all be subjects of His teaching, and under His guidance may be brought to the knowledge of Him whom to know is eternal life. Labour also to know whether we love the Lord Jesus Christ. Do we sing His glory with the angels, or publish the glad tidings with the shepherds, or rejoice with the wise men, and glad that we have felt the power of His grace in our hearts? Or are we, with Herod, troubled at the idea of His birth, and filled with anger at the mention of His name? These are tests. Do you exult in the prosperity of Christ's kingdom, or are you uneasy at its progress in the world? When religion comes near home, and offers to lay its restraints on our hearts—to injure our worldly interests, or endanger our personal care—do we rejoice, or are we troubled? Let us not crucify the Lord of glory, but welcome Him to our souls. Let us not put Him to open shame by our sins, but magnify Him as the Prince of Peace, and establish His throne in our hearts.

SERMON II.

"Christ is all in all."—HEBREWS i. 9.

"THEREFORE God, even thy God, hath anointed thee with the oil of gladness, above thy fellows."

By the phrase, "God, even thy God," we are to understand God the Father. Such expressions are often employed in Holy Scripture. "The Lord said unto my Lord;" and again, "The Lord rained upon Sodom and Gomorrah brimstone and fire from the Lord out of heaven."

By "the oil of gladness" is here meant the Holy Spirit. That this should be so, is prophesied in the Old Testament, and confirmed in the New. "The Spirit of the Lord is upon me, because He hath anointed me to preach the gospel to the poor; he hath sent me to heal the broken-hearted, to preach deliverance to the captives, and recovering of sight to the blind, to set at liberty them that are bruised, to preach the acceptable year of the Lord." Sometimes the operation of God's Holy Spirit is compared to water, which cleanses; at other times, to fire, which purifies; in this place, to oil, which softens the heart, and makes our yoke easy.

By "gladness" is to be understood the fruit of the Spirit, such as, "love, joy, peace, gentleness, goodness, and faith. It is a foretaste of greater things to come. "Well done, thou good and faithful servant, enter thou into the joy of thy Lord." "In thy presence there is fulness of joy; at thy right hand there are pleasures for evermore." By "thy fellows" is signified all those true Christians who have been made kings and priests unto God, partakers of the same Spirit, recipients of the same joy; in nature the same, in degree less. He, having all fulness; they, only by measure. By His divine nature, He was equal with the Father. "Awake, O sword, against my Shepherd, against the man who is my Fellow, saith the Lord of Hosts." Again, by His human nature, He was truly man. "Forasmuch as the children are partakers of flesh and blood, so also himself likewise took part of the same." A wonderful union of blessed Trinity. God the Father had anointed thee, God the "Son, with the oil of gladness—God the Holy Ghost— "above thy fellows." This is Christ's Church.

Let us here inquire:—

1. What is meant by the anointing spoken of—" God hath anointed thee."

II. The end for which our Lord was anointed.

III. The lesson it teaches, and the blessings we reap.

Under the law the ceremony of anointing consisted of three essentials :—1. Being set apart by God. 2. A meetness for the office. 3. Having holy oil actually poured on the head.

I. So our blessed Saviour was set apart for the great work of redemption. He had been chosen from all eternity, by "the determinate counsel and foreknowledge of God," to effect the salvation of man. He did not thrust Himself into the office as an usurper, but assumed it according to the express appointment of the Father. As no man should take the honour of the priesthood unto himself, except he who was called of God, as Aaron, so also Christ glorified not himself, to be made an high priest, but He who said unto Him, " Thou art my Son, this day have I begotten thee," also ordained Him to the office. He did not take it by force, but assumed its sacred functions in accordance to the Divine will. Christ himself thus saith, " I am not come of myself, but He who sent me is true, whom you know not." In the same strain, soon after His death, St Peter lets " all the house of Israel know assuredly that God had made that same Jesus, whom they had crucified, both Lord and Christ." That He who was Christ the Lord should not undertake so important a charge, so great and necessary a work, as the salvation of lost souls, until duly commissioned of the Father, teaches us to be cautious how we should engage in the like service, unless directed from the same source. In one place we read of a person who came to Christ, requesting Him "to divide the inheritance between him and his brother," and He said unto him, "Man, who made me a judge or a divider among you?" He could have discharged the office of a judge, as well as that of a physician; to decide cases of law as easy as to remove the disease of the body. But this was not His commission. No one could taunt Him, insolently asking, "Who made thee a ruler and a judge over us." He kept within His allotted sphere, and exceeded not the bounds of His own province. With a gentle reproof He condemns this spirit in others, saying, "What is that to thee, follow thou me,"—cease to pry into other's concerns, be diligent in thine own calling. When a river gently glides along its wonted channels, its waters are clear and wholesome, but when it overflows its banks, it often commits great damages. Whilst we keep within the limits assigned us, we prosper and succeed. When we stray from the path of duty, and exceed the bounds of our own calling, we generally go wrong, and do great mischief. It would be well were all to follow our blessed Saviour as their ensample, as well as their teacher, to be contented with their lot, and useful in their stations.

God's people of old, whose deeds are recorded to their honour, and whose efforts were everywhere crowned with success, would never engage in any undertaking unless they were first truly convinced of their calling, evidenced by a divine testimony. This, which accounts for their great success, accounts also for our failures. "God said unto Moses, thus shalt thou say unto the children of Israel: The Lord God of your fathers, the God of Abraham, the God of Isaac, the God of Jacob, hath sent me unto you." David had been assured that "God had made him the head of the heathen." Jeremiah, speaking of himself, declares, "As for me, I have not hastened from being a pastor to follow thee." Amos is not ashamed to own before the king, "I was no prophet, neither was I a prophet's son; but I was an herdman, and a gatherer of sycamore fruit: And the Lord took me as I followed the flock, and the Lord said unto me, Go, prophesy unto my people

Israel." This plain shepherd was far more successful in his ministry than all the priests at Bethel, and why?—Because he had been sent of God.

2. The anointing under the law signified that the persons so anointed were worthy and fit for the office, and endowed with every gift and grace to discharge their duties thoroughly and effectually. So Jesus is called CHRIST the Anointed. The gifts and the graces of the Spirit had been poured upon Him without measure. He was mighty to save. One saith in Isaiah, "Make me not a ruler of the people, for in my house is neither bread nor clothing." Princes should be rich. If they are poor, they will oppress their subjects, and wrest them of their possessions. Our help was not laid upon one faint with toil, or weary with fatigue, but was on Him in whom all fulness dwelt—irresistible in power, triumphant in victory, and more than a conqueror. As Samson rose at midnight, and carried the gates of Gaza to the top of a high hill, even so our victorious Redeemer arose from the grave, and having spoiled the territories of death and hell, He ascended in triumph into heaven. "Wherefore, He is able to save them to the uttermost that come unto God by Him, seeing He ever liveth to make intercession for them." Our

great High Priest is not like the high priests of old; though touched with the feelings of our infirmities, He has no infirmity of His own. His word is faithfulness and truth. Before Him the powers of darkness flee abashed; sin and destruction are conquered foes. What a source of joy to every believer, that his Saviour, who is Christ the Lord, can accomplish what He hath undertaken, and finish what He hath begun. The leper's consolation sprang from Christ's power,—" If thou wilt, thou *canst* make me clean." Soul, thou hast a God worthy of thy trust. His willingness to help thee is as great as His power to save thee. Seeing He is almighty, rest on His all-sufficiency, and put your whole trust in His mercy. Let men run here and there for support in their trials, and comfort in their disappointments; but let true Christians trust in Christ, bow with cheerful resignation to His will, rest with implicit confidence on His merits, and shew to the outward world the true source of their inward joy. In every trial trust in Him; He can preserve Moses in an ark of bulrushes, as well as save Noah in an ark of gopher-wood. He can deliver by means, without means, and against means. " If He be for us, who can be against us?" Our salvation is in His hand, we are kept by His power. In the time of man's innocency, Adam's happiness was entrusted to his own charge, but he forfeited the charge, and lost the privilege. Now our salvation is placed in One who is mighty, yea, almighty to save, and who can pluck it out of His hands? Believer, all thine enemies, which disturb thy peace, and distress thy soul, shall be destroyed for ever. They shall be broken "with a rod of iron," and be dashed "in pieces like a potter's vessel," and thy refuge is beyond the reach of their darts.

3. Under the law it was customary to anoint with material oil. "Samuel took a phial of oil, and poured it upon the head of Saul." "The young prophet poured oil on the head of Jehu." The Captain of our Salvation was not anointed with material oil, but with the Holy Ghost— the oil of gladness, of which material oil was only a type and shadow. This is the true oil, which humbles our pride, subdues our spirits, and stamps divine impressions on the heart. When this oil is poured on our consciences, it awakens our souls, and quickens our deadness, making us "fervent in spirit, serving the Lord." Of Samson it is said, that when "the Spirit of the Lord came mightily upon him," he performed some wonderful deeds. Of the disciples we read, that when "the Spirit appeared unto them like cloven tongues, as of fire, and sat upon each of them," they were instantly pro-

claiming the wonderful works of God in divers languages, as the Spirit gave them utterance. O ye " slow of heart," who can neither bear this fire of conviction, nor yet escape the force of its truth, pray God that His Spirit's influence may touch your heart, and your souls, " before you are aware, shall be made like the chariots of Aminadab." This oil cheers the soul more than anything else under the sun. The worldling may rejoice in his gains, and the sensual revel in his lust, but the pleasures of both are momentary, and are often attended with sorrow and shame; but he who receives this oil experiences that inward joy and "gladness of heart, more than in the time" their schemes prospered, and "their corn and wine increased." When the eunuch had tasted of this oil, " he went his way rejoicing." When Samaria had received it, the city " was glad." Paul and Silas, having richly partaken of this oil of gladness, sang praises at midnight in the dungeon. Ye who are merry, and rejoice at the public-house, but downcast and drowsy in the house of prayer, come and partake of this Spirit, that your lives may be changed and your souls may be saved.

II. The end for which our Lord was anointed. This unction shadowed forth the nature of

His office. Under the law, prophets, priests, and kings were anointed with oil. Some had filled two offices together, as Melchisedec, who was both king and priest. David was a prophet and a king. Jeremiah was a priest and a prophet. But He who had been anointed with the oil of gladness above His *fellows*, was invested with the three offices of prophet, priest, and king—a prophet to teach us, a priest to intercede for us, and a king to rule over us.

As a prophet He was to teach us His Father's will. This had been early foretold of Him; "for Moses truly said unto the fathers, a prophet shall the Lord your God raise up unto you of your brethren, like unto me; him shall ye hear in all things whatsoever he shall say unto you." Other prophets only in part, but He hath declared unto us the whole counsel of God. Hence He is called "the Great Prophet" of His Church, mighty in word and in deed. Attend to His instructions, treasure them up in your hearts, for the "soul that will not hear Him shall be destroyed from among the people." To Him we should "give the more earnest heed, for if the word spoken by angels was stedfast, and every transgression and disobedience received a just recompense of reward, how shall we escape if we neglect so great a salvation."

"He is the way, the truth, and the life;" walk ye therein, and be ye saved."

Jesus was also anointed to be a priest. The Lord hath sworn, and will not repent: "Thou art a priest for ever, after the order of Melchisedec." As a high priest, His office consisted of two things, viz., making atonement for sin, and making intercession for man. Under the law, when any one sinned, he was to bring an offering unto the priest, who was to offer it for him. When we have sinned against heaven and earth, our sins can only be expiated by the sacrifice which Jesus offered for sinners. "By one offering He hath perfected for ever them that are sanctified." And if our sins be not cleansed in His blood, there "remaineth no more sacrifice for sin." The priests of old would not part with one drop of their own blood for the best of the people, but He shed the blood of His heart for the vilest of men.

The other part of the priestly office consisted in making intercession. This He is well qualified to discharge, seeing He ever liveth to intercede for us. "We have an Advocate with the Father, Jesus Christ the righteous." Many are unfaithful to their trust because they are not righteous in their ways, but He who is our great High Priest is righteous in all His ways, and faithful in all His promises—all creatures are tender to their own nature. The bear will not be easily robbed of her young. Our great High Priest took upon Him our nature, that He might be touched with a feeling of our infirmities." He loved His own, and loves them to the end. They are one with Him and He with them, members of His body, children of His Father, co-heirs and joint heirs with himself. For their sake He endured the penalties of sin, the pains of sin, and the agonies of the cross. Though now exalted to the right hand of the Majesty on high, yet He hath still His eyes upon His people, and His ears open to their prayers. He sympathizes with the weary, and feels for the heavy laden.

Of His kingly office there can be no doubt. God declares of Him, "I have set my King upon my holy hill of Zion." This had also been foretold of Him in a very explicit manner by the angelic annunciation, "He shall be great, and shall be called the Son of the Highest; and the Lord God shall give Him the throne of his father, David, and He shall reign over the house of Jacob for ever, and of His kingdom there shall be no end." His kingdom was not of this world. In this world there must be subjects before there can be a sovereign, but in the kingdom of Christ it is not so. He chooses His people, and not the people their king. He hath not one subject who is not drawn by the power of His grace. "Other sheep," saith He, "I have who are not of this fold; them also I must bring, and they shall hear my voice, and there shall be one fold and one shepherd." Were we to find a kingdom free from all inconveniences, and abounding with all advantages, who would not force his way to enjoy its privileges? We know that the kingdom of Christ is full of all such blessings as pertain to life here, and immortality hereafter, yet years elapse before we are within the true fold. He waits to be gracious. His long-suffering, tenderness, and compassion, yearn for our adoption. Though He often finds us asleep, yet He comes and awakens us; He leads us through the iron gates of difficulties, delivers us from thousand dangers, and never rests, until, through Him, we reach the eternal city—His kingdom in heaven. Often we are betrayed to fear, but as long as He reigneth, everything shall work together for its good; and whether of dominion, power, extent, or duration, "of His kingdom there shall be no end." In a clock there are several wheels, which run counter to one another, some move slowly, others whirl about with great quickness; yet all unite in keeping the clock in motion, and contribute their share to make a true index of the flight of time. Even so is every event, however opposite it may seem, disposed by the secret, impelling hand of God, to promote His glory and further the salvation of His people. This is wonderfully illustrated: "When our Lord was entered into a ship, His disciples followed Him, and, behold, there arose a great tempest in the sea, insomuch that the ship was covered with the waves: but He was asleep. But when He awoke, He rebuked the wind and the waves, and there was a great calm." The disciples seemed so astonished at the effect produced, that it is said "they marvelled, and said, What manner of man is this, that even the winds and the sea obey Him?" Jacob once complained, "Joseph is not, and Simeon is not; and ye will take Benjamin away: all these things are against me." Yet, though old, it was not so, for he saw them all again in comfort and prosperity, which made his heart rejoice.

Our blessed Saviour is a King who protects His people, and fights for His subjects. "Gird thy sword upon thy thigh, O thou most Mighty;" and in the vision granted to St John, He is described "as clothed with a vesture dipped in blood." Angels are amazed at this sight, and ask in astonishment, "Who is this with dyed garments?" These garments He wears as a badge to His people. When they rest, He fights; when they are mourning over your sins,

He is conquering principalities in their behalf. He not only fights with them, but also for them. "Fear not, stand still, and see the salvation of the Lord, for He fighteth for you." This consideration, which affords sweet comfort to the godly, should strike terror into the heart of the wicked; if sinners resist His will, saying, "we will not have this man to reign over us," they shall be suddenly destroyed, and that without remedy; if they continue their cry, "let us break His bands asunder, and cast His cords from us," there will come a day, when He will "break them with a rod of iron, and dash them in pieces like a potter's vessel." "Kiss the Son, lest He be angry;" bow the knee to the sceptre of His grace, lest ye be consumed in the midst of your sins.

When we, through sin, were cut off from the favour of God, He took upon Him our nature, that He might reconcile us unto himself, and now, by His Spirit, applies that reconciliation to our souls. Under this dispensation of grace He appears under three different characters, still it is the same God, rich in mercy and infinite in love. This is one of the deep mysteries of the Gospel-divine essences which can no more be separated than heat, light, and air;— the three great essentials of fire. Human wisdom can never comprehend this truth, yet human souls believe through faith on the eternal I Am, who hath revealed it. To maintain this doctrine in all its essentials is a matter of the greatest consequence, as our eternal salvation stands or falls therewith. We must insist upon this grand peculiarity of the Christian religion, as it is the foundation of all our hopes. Let others triumph in the notion of their superior knowledge, we will simply adhere to the doctrines of the Bible, and not presume to be wise above what is written. Let our sole aim to be like this triune God. Nothing can make us resemble God more than having God's grace, " to love our enemies, to bless them that curse us, and do good to them that hate us." A mother will leave for a moment her dying child, to rescue a beast from perishing. God, who prefers mercy before sacrifice, will dispense with His own worship, while a sheep, fallen into a pit, is lifted out.

2. Consider the inestimable blessings and the high privileges to which Christians are entitled through this anointing. They assume Christ's name, and through Him become partakers of the same blessings. They too are anointed. " As the precious ointment which was poured upon the head of Aaron ran down his beard, and went down to the skirts of his garments," even so the oil of gladness, wherewith our Lord Jesus

was anointed, ran, and still continues to run down, to bless and enrich the meanest of His people. May we be so united by faith to our living Head, that, being "His fellows," we may not only be called after His name, but be made partakers of His grace. May the oil of gladness, distilling from His anointed head, drop by drop, be poured into our souls, until, having received of "His fulness, and grace for grace," that we may not merely profess His name, but bear His image.

Seeing, then, that the Father hath anointed the Son, we should also anoint Him. We may anoint His feet with our tears. It is said of one that "she washed His feet with her tears, and wiped them with the hair of her head." Tears of true penitents are precious in God's sight, so precious, indeed, that it is said of Him, "Thou puttest my tears in thy bottle." Many complain of hard times—few complain of hard hearts. Many weep for the losses they sustain—few mourn for their souls which perish. Christ shed the blood of His heart for the sins of others—will you not weep for your own? Tears which spring from a broken and a contrite heart procure peace which the world cannot give, and inherit a blessing the world cannot bestow. "Blessed are they that mourn, for they shall be comforted."

We may anoint His head with the affection of

true love. "Love is the fulfilling of the law." It is the richest treasure which God bestows, and the sweetest grace which we can possess. Other persons and things we may love too much, but He who is anointed of the Father may love too little. "Mary loved much," but not too much. Angels cannot sufficiently love Him who is love. The Church, unable to recount His manifold excellences, sums up the whole in this brief summary, "He is altogether lovely." The more we love Him, the more we shall continue to love Him. It is the essence of the Godhead, for "God is love." May this love be shed abroad in our hearts, and transform us to the likeness of His Son. May it kindle in our souls a flame, that we may love Him who is the "chief among ten thousand," with an ardour which many waters cannot quench, and the floods of persecution cannot drown. When we truly love Him who is anointed of the Father, we shall also love them who are anointed of Him, and be kindly affectioned one to another.

We should also, like Nicodemus, anoint His body. This is done by compassion, pity, and tenderness, shewn towards those who are "His *fellows*,"—being true Christians. This is the most fragrant ointment that can be poured on Him. They are flesh of His flesh, and bone of His bone. Neither distance, poverty, nor time, can dissolve the union cemented by love, centred in Him, still subsisting between Him and His people. He weeps with them that weep, and rejoices with them that rejoice. Every wrong done unto them He deems as an injury inflicted upon himself,—"Saul, Saul, why persecutest thou me?" "Inasmuch as ye have not done it unto them, ye have not done it to me." In proportion as God hath blessed us we should prove a blessing to others, and though without faith no work can be pleasing in His sight, yet our faith must be seen by our works, appear in our life and conversation. The woman who poured ointment on His head will have the deed proclaimed "for a memorial of her, wheresoever the Gospel shall be preached." He who counts up your tears, also reckons in His book your good works and godly deeds. On that august and awful theatre of the last day, He will proclaim to a whole universe all the secrets of your hearts, every mite you have given to His service, every journey you have taken to His house, every back you have clothed, every need you have allayed, every tear you have shed, and every prayer you have offered. If you have tasted of the oil of gladness in your souls, you will honour the Lord with your substance, and anoint His body, His members in need, with the first-fruit of your increase. May it please Him who was anointed of the Father, through His Holy Spirit, to bless your life, and save your souls! Amen.

SERMON III.

"Moreover, if thy brother shall trespass against thee, go and tell him his fault between thee and him alone : if he shall hear thee, thou hast gained thy brother."—MATTH. xviii. 15.

Our blessed Saviour, having before warned His disciples against giving offence, here directs them how to deal with those who have offended them. If thy brother trespass against thee, either by falsehood or injury, damaging thy reputation, or insulting thy person, or in any manner that hurts thy feelings, or grieves thy soul, then the rule is, "go and tell him his fault." Never reproach him in his absence, or speak ill of him to others. Let no hatred root in thine heart, nor any malice rancour in thy bosom. "Go not forth hastily to strive, lest thou know not what to do in the end. Debate thy cause with thy neighbour himself, and discover not a secret to another."

Here we propose, with the divine assistance, to show:—

I. *Whom* we are to reprove—" If thy brother."

II. *Why* we are to reprove—" Shall trespass against thee."

III. *How* we are to reprove—" Go and tell him his fault."

IV. The object of our reproof—" If he shall hear thee, thou hast gained thy brother."

I. Whom we are to reprove—our brother. In a general sense, every man is our brother. "God hath made of one blood all nations of men, for to dwell on all the face of the earth." God also highly resents every breach of brotherly affection, and promises signal blessings on brotherly love. Through the prophet Amos, God declares, "For three transgressions of Edom, and for four I will not turn away the punishment thereof, because he did pursue his brother with a sword, and did cast off all pity, and his anger did tear perpetually, and he kept his wrath for ever." Though "brother" implies every individual, yet there is a *peculiar* sense in which the term is still employed, and in which the word "brother" is yet to be understood. By "brother," our Saviour might probably here mean one of His own disciples, one bound to Him, and united to us by stronger ties than that of blood. Having been created by God the Father, begotten again to a new life by God the Holy Ghost, our blessed

Saviour is not ashamed to call such His brethren, and any kindness done to the least of them He reckons as done to himself. "We are one body and one spirit, even as we are called in one hope of our calling." We have "one Lord, one faith, one baptism," holding the same views, sharing in the same privileges, and look forward to the same inheritance, the same rest, and the same joys." "We," saith the apostle, "are the body of Christ, and members in particular." As in the natural body, the members have the same care one for another, that when one member suffers, all the members suffer with it. When the foot is hurt, the eyes examine the wound, the ears attend to the orders given, and the hands apply the remedy prescribed. We should rescue our brother from all dangers, bear his burdens, and relieve his necessities. Connive not at his sin, warn him freely, and, if it be necessary, rebuke him sharply. Pursue the path of duty. "Be stedfast, unmovable, always abounding in the work of the Lord," and your labour shall never be in vain.

II. We are to shew *why*, or for what, we are to reprove our brother. "If thy brother trespass against thee." This seems to characterise the offence, yet the offence is very grave, for it includes not only personal offences and temporal disadvantages, but likewise every sin committed against God, and every evil done against our neighbour. Every true Christian seems far more concerned for the honour and glory of God than for any insult levelled against himself, and feels for others as much as he feels for himself. Moses was as much grieved at Israel's sins, as if he had himself been guilty of their crimes. "If thou wilt not," said he, "forgive their sin, blot me, I pray thee, out of thy book." And St Paul declares the same truth. "Who is weak, and I am not weak, who is offended, and I burn not? Our brother's trespasses, when allowed to go unreproved, not only dishonour God, injure our neighbour, wound ourselves, but also threaten to involve us in his punishment. For Achan's sin thirty-six men were slain. For the sin of Eli's sons many in Israel fell, and the ark of God was taken. For David's sin in numbering the people, no less than seventy thousand died of the pestilence. The sins of individuals affect the whole community, it leavens the whole lump, and at length ruins the whole fabric. It shuts the windows of heaven, clouds drop not their fatness, the earth yields not her increase, famine begins her work, judgment begins to fall, and terrible desolation sweeps through the land. Seeing, then, these fearful consequences, which ensue from our negligences, ought we not to reprove our brother's trespasses? "Go and tell him his faults between thee and him alone?"

III. How we are to reprove—"go and tell him his fault." This is no easy task, and needs great wisdom and much grace. A few rules for our guidance, both in the exercise and discharge of our duty, we shall here lay down.

1. Ascertain, beyond all doubts, that the person whom we are to reprove is actually guilty of the sin laid to his charge. Until you have obtained the clearest evidence of his guilt, intrude not with any proffered services. This the text implies—"if thy brother trespass against thee." Let the charge be first proved. Let no idle report prejudice thy judgment, and let no prejudice bias thy mind. Evil tongues carry evil tidings. When the accused is found innocent, the accusers rather grieve he is not guilty, than rejoice at his innocence and acquittal. Such are "witnesses against their neighbours without a cause." If you would reprove with propriety, be cautious how you condemn hastily. Remember that "love thinketh no evil." Use no harshness, nay, take heed lest you fall. Weigh well the evidence, examine the test of its truth, consider long the charge, the nature of the fault, and the degree of its malignity, and let the

gentleness of your reproof be tempered with all the tenderness of love.

2. The prophet, when he proclaims, "that the soul which sinneth shall die," does not specify any particular sin, knowing that every sin deserves death. Yet when we compare sins together, some appear light, others seem aggravated, and marked with great enormity. This distinction is shewn in our Lord's testimony before Pilate, " he who delivered me unto thee hath the greater sin;" and the same sentiment is expressed in the text, " thou hast gained thy brother." He could not have been gained unless he had been lost. One is not lost when he yields to natural infirmities, to which we are all subject, and which are inseparable from our imperfect state. " In many things we all offend." The sin for which we should dare reprove our brother should not consist of those small offences, or of light nature, but of an aggravated character, as needed severe discipline, such as Church censure and Church excommunication.

3. The physician seldom administers his medicines when all hopes of recovery are past, much more should he forbear when he knows they would do more harm than good. You should likewise spare your reproofs when more likely to prove injurious rather than beneficial.

It is better not to labour than to labour to no purpose. To reprove some persons is worse than lost labour. It only serves to confirm their prejudice, to establish their resentment, and rekindle their anger. An enraged madman, or a blasphemous scoffer, you do wiser to avoid than attempt to reprove. Abigail never reproved Nabal for his rash and scornful reply to David's young men. She knew that to admonish his enraged bosom at the time would be only adding fuel to the fire, and rekindling the spark, just allayed, to burn with greater force and fury. In some instances the best efforts utterly fail. Hence we hear the complaint in Ezekiel's prophecy, "Son of Man, the house of Israel is to me become dross; all they are brass, and tin, and iron, and lead, in the midst of the furnace." There they lie melting, and if the heat of the furnace remove not the dross, nothing can. We should then seek wisdom from above, and pray for the Spirit's teaching that you may know *whom* and *how* to reprove, lest you injure the cause you are endeavouring to serve. "Give not that which is holy unto the dogs, neither cast ye your pearls before swine: lest they trample them under their feet, and turn again, and rend you." To reprove profitably, needs all the work of a cool head and a gracious heart. It is the peculiar province of a good man, for none but a good man will truly feel and really grieve for the wickedness of the wicked. When you reprove, go to your brother in the spirit of meekness, and deal as tenderly with him as if you were going to probe an instrument into a deep wound. It needs the utmost delicacy, and requires the truest sympathy. When Elijah was concealing himself from the vengeance of Jezebel, in a cave on Mount Horeb, a spirit of despair embittered his soul; the persecution he was suffering caused a cry of complaint, and in a fit of despondency he spoke unadvisedly with his lips. His zeal had been great for the Lord, but now his soul had sunk in despair, and he longed to die; at this time he felt the gentle touch of an angel's hand, and heard the gentle reproof of his voice, saying, " What doest thou here?" Go forth and stand upon the mount before the Lord, and, behold, the Lord passed by, and a great wind rent the mountains, and brake in pieces the rocks, and after the wind an earthquake, and after the earthquake, fire, and after the fire, a still small voice."

Thus God shewed that He had many means, both terrible and awful, whereby He might destroy the strongest, and make the stoutest tremble, to humble the mind and bow the heart; but in this instance He calmed the prophet's ruffled spirit by His tender pity—the still small voice—

rather than by the loud and alarming displays of His majesty.

Some men's reproofs are violent and vehement, like a whirlwind, tearing all to pieces, and by its force driving the brother to greater ruin. Others are so sudden and cutting, like an earthquake, they rend the conscience, and inflict wounds with fresh sores, exposed and unhealed. Others, again, having more zeal than knowledge, like fire, consume the very existence of hope, rather than enlighten the mind and save the soul. But God is in none of these. His reproofs come with a gentleness and tenderness, blended with meekness and compassion, which move all the inner feelings, and by the load of a brother's sympathy draws out a brother's soul. Be wise in your admonitions, and gentle in your reproofs. May God's Spirit lead you to the knowledge of all truth, and direct you in the performance of all duty!

When you are about to reprove a brother, do not send for him, nor write to him, or wait for him, but go to him. This will convince your brother that your heart is not estranged from him, nor your sympathy closed against him. Seek an opportunity for the occasion in the same manner, and from the same source as you seek wisdom for the work.

God did not call our first parents to an account

of their transgression till the cool of the day—till they saw their nakedness, and the miserable condition to which sin had reduced them—not until then did He appear amongst the trees of the garden, to reason with them for their conduct, and to reason with them for their sin. As "there is a time to speak, and a time to keep silence," so there is a time to reprove, and to forbear reproving. There is a time in which the transgression of the wicked may be manifold, and their sins mighty; a time in which they may afflict, take a bribe, and turn aside the poor in the gate from their right; in that time the prudent will keep silence, for it is an evil time. It is never wise to draw a sword against a madman, nor venture to sea in a storm. When the spies brought back an evil report respecting the land of promise, there was a great tumult created in the camp, and great indignation expressed against Moses and Aaron; but they "fell on their faces before all the assembly of the congregation of Israel," and while they were thus prostrate on the ground, their fury ceased, and their rage cooled down. There are, therefore, seasons for reproofs, and all unseasonable reproof will be an ineffectual reproof.

" Tell your brother his fault between you and him alone." If his trespass was secret, do not make it public : bury his sin in your own bosom.

Try to heal his soul without wounding his fame. When Joseph's bowels yearned to make himself known to his brethren, gently reproving them of their unkindness, he suffered none to be present but his brethren and himself. When God reproved Aaron and Miriam for their murmuring against Moses, he called them into the tabernacle, causing them to withdraw from the open eye and the open ear. Private faults should have private hearing; expose not his weakness, and publish not his faults. Let the glory of God, the hatred of sin, and the salvation of your brother's soul, be your chief aim. Stimulated by such motives, and guided by such a spirit, " go to him and tell him plainly, unfold his crime before him, point out its nature, its aggravation, and its awful consequences, and with unmistakable earnestness, blended with unfeigned compassion, ask him, is not this sin? Is not this crucifying again the Son of God? Does it not wound the conscience, endanger the soul, and dishonour God? A milder course, and softer accents, would too much resemble Eli's conduct, who only said to his sons, " Why do ye so?" Spare not your reproofs when the truth is in danger. Paul withstood Peter to his face. Nathan shewed no favour to David. Elijah told Ahab, " where the dogs licked the blood of Naboth, shall dogs lick thy blood." Nehemiah charged Sanballat,

"Thou hast," said he, touching Sanballat's falsehood, "feigned them out of thine own heart." Such intrepid reprovers are not often found. Such reproofs are valuable and wholesome. They restrain bad actions, they encourage good works; they stem the tide of sin, and further the salvation of man; they promote the glory of God, and extend the kingdom of Christ; they secure peace on earth, and goodwill amongst men.

SERMON IV.

"And he said unto Jesus, Lord, remember me when thou comest into thy kingdom. And Jesus said unto him, To-day shalt thou be with me in paradise."—LUKE xxiii. 42, 43.

IN this, as well as in many other instances, we possess abundant evidence of God's free grace, as manifested towards mankind. The woman of Samaria furnishes a wonderful instance of divine grace. She had nothing to deserve the least favour. She neither offered to draw the water from the well to quench His thirst, nor made the least effort to refresh His weary limbs. Yet, by God's grace, this person, once lost in infamy and sin, tasted of the living water, and was the first to proclaim the glad tidings in the city of Samaria.

Also, Mary Magdalene and Saul of Tarsus were remarkable instances of divine grace. Yet one probably had witnessed many of the Lord's miracles, and the other had seen a light from heaven; but of the thief on the cross, he had seen no miracles, and heard no voice from heaven. He was nailed to the fatal tree, and, drawing near the end of his fatal course, had nothing presented to his view but a crucified Saviour—a mangled body, and a pierced side, yet in a few minutes he was converted—converted from a thief to a martyr, and taken from the gallows into paradise. What wonders of grace! A man sentenced to the cross, in the twinkling of an eye, is changed into a saint—makes public profession of faith in his Redeemer expiring on the same tree, and is for ever absolved from all his sins. The Preacher saith that "there is a time to be born, and a time to die: a time to plant, and a time to pluck up that which is planted: a time to kill, and a time to heal: a time to break down, and a time to build up: a time to weep, and a time to laugh." Now, all these contrary schemes God's wisdom unite into one, and centre together in the conversion of the thief. At one and the same time, behold, he is born into Christ, and is dying to the world. Grace is planted in the soul, and sin is taken up by the roots. The Son of God expiring on the cross gives life to the dying thief. With Christ's stripes, then received, the sins of his heart were for ever forgiven. When the body of death was broken down, the work of grace was built up. When he was weeping for his sins, he was rejoicing that he should be soon with Jesus in paradise. St Chrysostom declares this to be the greatest of miracles. The darkening of the sun is not so great as enlightening the understanding. The cleaving of the rocks is not compared to the softening of the heart; the rending of the veil of the temple, with the removal of the veil of darkness, which keeps the soul in the shadow of death.. Moses' rod, the authority of his divine mission, well confirms this truth. Every creature seemed subject to its authority —it divided the sea, it smote the earth—light was under its control, and darkness felt its sway; but on Pharaoh's heart it produced no effect, and exercised no control. It is easier to tear the rock in pieces than make one heart,—hardened in sin,—contrite, broken, and penitent. Satan might say, that in the hour of temptation he had seduced the twelve disciples, yet Christ shews that He can rescue in the hour of death. It is said that Solomon fought against the Egyptians with their own horses. So doth the Church confound the enemies of the cross of Christ, and make their death redound to His glory. Here is a triumph, where the Captain of our salvation was more than a conqueror, and victory which none but Jesus could achieve.

Here we also perceive amazing humility. It was an astonishing act of condescension that he should " take upon him the form of a man," but greater that he should assume "the form of a servant;" greater still, that he became "a worm and no man;" but greatest than all, that he should die like a thief between two thieves. Behold the love of Christ! he accepts the tongue of a thief to proclaim His divinity, and permits it to establish His innocency. An angel's voice or a prophet's tongue he might employ to proclaim His glory, but he chose a thief's tongue, that, from the meanness of the instrument, His power should be more apparent and His glory more exalted. See also here infinite *compassion.* Behold the Lord of Life pouring out the blood of His heart amongst two thieves, that He might expiate the guilt of one of them. When a tree has grown crooked, leaning altogether to one side, it is likely, in the end, to fall in that direction. But here is a man, whose downward course all his life-long pointed strongly towards hell, yet when he comes to be cut down, things are reversed, and he is taken up to heaven. Not only are his crooked ways made straight and his perverse will subdued, but his soul is sanctified, and made fit for the inheritance of the saints in light. In an instant this man was conducted through every operation of grace, and brought not merely to lay hold by faith on the promises, but into actual possession of eternal life.

Saving one thief, and leaving the other to perish, savours much of election by grace; but God's judgments are very secret and unsearchable. We should neither doubt nor dispute about them, but rather reverence His ways, and hallow His most holy name. Pharaoh and Nebuchadnezzar were equally blessed with the means of grace, but the same means produced different effect. The one was hardened, the other was humbled. They were both men of the same nature, occupying the same station; being kings, and guilty of the same crime, both had led the children of Israel into captivity. Both were visited with plagues from heaven, and both were alike admonished to know the rod, and Him who appointed it. One said, "Who is the Lord that I should obey him;" the other cried out, "I praise, and extol, and honour the King of Heaven." God loves to display His sovereign will. "I will," said He to Moses, "be gracious to whom I will be gracious, and will shew mercy on whom I will shew mercy." He will do what seemeth good in His sight. Where "two are in the field, one shall be taken, the other shall be left." Men who wish to do as they *please*, are often found disputing about the ways of God. Let us acknowledge only His name, and bow always to His will.

From the mercy extended to the one and withholden from the other, we learn that our safest way to heaven lies between hope and fear. Fear is the cable which lays hold on hope, and hope is the anchor which makes fear firm. Fear removes all self-confidence, knowing how unworthy we are of the least of God's mercies. Hope, again, inspires with confidence, knowing the goodness of God, how boundless He is in mercy, how matchless in His love. Upon these graces doth the Lord confer His blessing, and bestow His gifts. "He taketh pleasure in them who fear Him, in those who hope in His mercy." O believer, the way that leads unto life is safe, lying between hope and fear. The one preserves thee from presumption, the other keeps thee from despair. We fear lest we enter not into our rest; we hope, waiting for the coming of our Lord. These are two strong bulwarks, to fence us on each side, and to keep us in the narrow path. The one is the thief who was left to perish, the other is the thief who found favour with the Lord; the former should teach you to fear, the latter should teach you how to hope. Some may appear *near* heaven, while they stand on the brink of hell. Others seem to be verging on destruction, while God is drawing them to heaven. "Take heed to yourselves, watch and pray." Christ can deliver at the eleventh hour, and "save to the uttermost those who come unto God by Him."

St Ambrose saith that despair is the greatest of all sins, not as an offence against God, but as most dangerous to men. It bars their blessedness, and cuts off their salvation. It is the blackest on the list, and the worst in existence. Judas' sin in selling his Saviour was not equal to his guilt of despair, which made him think God like unto himself, without a will to change, and without a power to forgive. "Woe unto such, for they have gone into the way of Cain," imagining "their iniquity to be greater than can be pardoned." Wonderful, indeed, is God's grace; it brings life out of death, light out of darkness, and salvation of sinners from the condemnation of the Saviour. His mercy knows neither measure nor end. Despair not of His goodness, fear His wrath, and hope in His salvation.

Let us consider the great change which God's grace wrought in this man. His hands and feet were nailed to the cross, but all that he had he gave unto the Lord. Only his heart and tongue were at his disposal, and these he freely devoted to his Master's service. With his tongue he vindicated Christ's innocence, saying, "This man hath done nothing amiss;" and in his heart he loved his Redeemer, wishing to be with Him in paradise. Herein are confession and faith, and herein consists man's salvation. "If thou confess with thy mouth the Lord Jesus, and shalt believe in thine heart that God hath raised Him from the dead, thou shalt be saved."

He also bore witness against himself, saying, "We receive the due reward of our deeds." This is the penitent's true token of deep contrition. "They confess their transgression unto the Lord, and their iniquity they do not hide." How much better would it have been for Judas to admit his guilt, than asking "Is it I," forfeiting God's favour by seeming to be innocent. Acknowledging our guilt, and condemning our own deeds, are precious gifts of grace. Calling heaven and earth to witness against our sins, expressing our unworthiness to claim God as our Father, or call ourselves as His children, smiting upon our breast, and suing for mercy, have once opened the Father's arms, and will again open the doors of paradise. "If we confess our sins, He is faithful and just to forgive us our sins, and to cleanse from all unrighteousness." Again, we find that he prayed, "Lord, remember me when thou comest in thy kingdom." With tears in his eyes, with death in his face, and with eternity before him, he turns to his Redeemer, and with true, yet touching words, he pours out his heart, saying, "*Lord, remember me.*" Here is deep humility. He does not pray, remove my pains, and let my sufferings cease; though I have not the honour to die for thee, yet I die with thee; he asks not for the martyr's crown, nor seeks he for the honour of sitting on the right hand in glory; he does not assume the burning zeal of St John, saying, "Come, Lord Jesus;" nor, like the spirits under the altar, cry out, "How long, how long." Whether it be soon, or whether it be yet a long time, all his prayer is, "Remember me."

He had also strong faith. It might be said to exceed that of Abraham, Moses, or Isaiah. Abraham had received many, great, and precious promises. Moses had witnessed His presence in the burning bush, and Isaiah had seen the Lord sitting on His throne in glory. Of some it is said, that great was their faith, but great also were the miracles which they had witnessed; but the thief saw not the Lord on His throne, nor God in the bush,—witnessed not His miracles on earth, nor sat in His presence on the mount. It is said that he knew how He had been sold by Judas, and forsaken by His disciples. He heard their blasphemy, and understood their danger. Yet he believes in Jesus, in the face of every obstacle, and proclaims His glory in the depth of His humiliation. Some, who had seen the Lord raising the dead, were afterwards shaken in their faith; but this man beheld him nailed to the cross, and sinking under the pains of death. He believed in the resurrection of the dead, and prayed for that life in the hour of death. See how grace exceeds nature. His fellow-thief knew of no life but the present, and that life was all he wanted. "If thou be Christ," said he, "save thyself and us." If Thou hast any power, exert it in rescuing us from the cross, and restore thyself to liberty. On the contrary, the penitent thief believed that "his kingdom was not of this world," and earnestly prayed, that, when Christ should come to reign in His own kingdom, he might be graciously remembered.

Whilst hanging between heaven and earth, having no rest for his body, yet he trusted entirely in Christ. Daniel was calm in the lions' den, but he knew that God had sent His angels to close their mouths. David was full of confidence in the midst of Saul's army, but he knew that the Lord preserved him. But this man, when all circumstances seemed to conspire against him in the agony of death, when his Lord was expiring by his side, was full of hope, and reposed a calm, stedfast confidence in his redeeming God. Lastly, we perceive in this man that love which is strong as death. Though the Lamb of God was "dumb as a sheep under the shearer's hand," and though all His disciples had feared and fled, yet he rebukes his companion, admits the justice of their punishment, and makes a confession of Christ as the Son of God. Our Lord said to Peter, the greatest of the apostles, "Whither I go, thou canst not follow me now;" but to this man He saith, "This day thou shalt be with me in paradise." A testimony of his title to paradise, and a meetness for heaven, he in an instant receives. It pleased the Lord that Paul's conversion should be almost an instantaneous act, suddenly he was struck to the ground, suddenly he heard a voice from heaven. Yet some days passed between his conversion and his preaching; but this man was a confessor and martyr at the same time, confessing Christ before men, and preaching to his fellow-companion in death, saying, "Dost thou not fear God, seeing thou art in the same condemnation?" Thou needst not fear the law, thou needst not fear the Jews, more neither can do. But, oh, dost thou not fear God, He can yet do more. He hath still power to cast thy body and soul into hell. Learn hence, that all who possess that fear which is the beginning of wisdom, wish the same impression to be made on all men's souls. Knowing that there is bread enough in their

Father's house, they urge all to partake thereof, that they should nourish their souls, and preserve them to eternal life. Having tasted the sweetness of divine life in their own souls, they long that others also should become partakers of the same blessing. "Come," say they with the Psalmist, "and we will declare what the Lord hath done for our souls." The just receive often more than they ask for. The thief on the cross desired only to be *remembered*, and, behold, immediately paradise is promised him. The thief, who had not been working in the vineyard, yet at the eleventh hour received his reward, what, then, shall they receive who have borne the burden and heat of the day? This man on the day of his new birth was admitted into the region of bliss. Grace and glory flowed in upon him so rapidly, that, like a full tide, they at once brought him to the haven where he would be safe. Through God's grace a desire is excited in the soul for heavenly things, and by God's mercy the desire is at once realized. This man no sooner said, " Remember me," than all the riches of paradise were conferred upon him. O happy man! thy Judge not only released thee from thy bondage, delivered thee from thy fears, but bestowed upon thee, from the abundant riches of His grace, the reward of eternal life. This is God's way of dealing with men. Abraham asked only for a son, but God gave a son from whose loins, "as concerning the flesh, Christ came, who is over all, God blessed for ever." Solomon asked for so much wisdom as would enable him to discern between the good and the bad, but God gave him great riches and honours besides. The servant who owed his Lord "ten thousand talents" only desired a longer time, saying, "Have patience with me, and I will pay thee all. But his Lord had compassion upon him, and forgave him the whole debt." Well doth the Church pray in the collect for the twelfth Sunday after Trinity, "Almighty and everlasting God, who art wont to give more than either we desire or deserve."

SERMON V.

"And we know that all things work together for good to them that love God, to them who are the called according to His purpose."—ROMANS viii. 28.

As if the Apostle had said, besides the many consolations already imparted unto you, I have this also to add, that all things shall work together for your good. Holy Scripture is full of sweet consolations, and for every season of need there appears some promise of relief. "Many are the afflictions of the righteous, but the Lord delivereth him out of them all." He hath a deliverance for every distress. He will, with the temptation, make also a way to escape, that they may be able to bear it. God "increaseth our consolations in proportion as the sufferings of Christ abound in us." He is not sparing of them to His people, but gives them "good measure; pressed down, and running over."

"*We know*,"—the Apostle limits this knowledge to the people of God alone. It is a privilege to which the ungodly have no claim. " The natural man receiveth not the things of the Spirit of God, for they are foolishness unto him, neither can he know them, because they are spiritually discerned." The real blessings of the Christian religion are known only to those who possess them. This world's treasures may appear most valuable to them who possess them not, but the hidden treasures of Gospel truth are only known to those who have found them. " The hidden manna and the new name" are things known to none " save to them that receive them." Spiritual joys the worldling cannot understand, and the Christian's privileges he does not appreciate. The beast of the field can form no conception of man's rational enjoyments; if it can have plenty of corn and hay, it cares for nothing more. So the natural man can form no notion of the believer's sweet joys, his heavenly pursuits, and heavenly pleasures. If he can secure Esau's inheritance, the fatness of the land, the increase of his corn and wine, he is contented. Having no eyes to look towards heaven, and no heart to seek those things which are above, he grovels in the dust, and is under the serpent's curse. May God remove this veil, open their eyes, and bring them to the knowledge of the truth!

"*We know*," &c.—This is the parent of spiritual courage. A real persuasion that all things work together for our good is a most encouraging source. The hope of victory emboldens the soldier; the prospect of gain encourages the sailor: yet neither knows the end. Blind as to the future, they cannot tell the result; but believers do not run with such uncertainty. Among all sorts of men which can be named, none have the like promises. When David had been deprived of all his prosperity, " he still encouraged himself in the Lord," and soon all things were restored to him. Learn we from hence, that, when true believers have been deprived of all their worldly goods, they have still a God to trust. To Him they may pour out their complaints, and from Him they expect deliverance; and whilst they can approach Him as *their* God, they will lack no good thing. Under their greatest losses, and in their greatest distresses, they have a promise, that, in their severest trials, they shall not be forsaken. " Though they fall, they shall yet arise." In their utmost straits, God is their refuge, and a very present help in trouble. His presence goes with them, and wherever they are there He is also. To such as are Israelites indeed He saith, " I will go with you, and give you rest." " Them that are meek shall He guide in judgment; and such as are gentle, shall He learn His way." He will "lead them forth by the right way, that they may go to a city of habitation." Sometimes they are led by His Word, which is "a lamp unto their feet, and a light unto their paths." At other times, by His providence; "our way is hedged in with thorns," lest we wander in the way, and be lost on our journey. Doubts *about* the way are often more perplexing, and more to be dreaded than dangers *on* the way. If assaulted by temptations on the way, our hearts should be thankful that we meet them *there,* as it would be death to meet them elsewhere. He will conceal us from dangers, and protect us from the enemy's darts. "Thou art their hiding place, thou shalt preserve them from trouble." Moses well knew the value of God's presence when he said, "If thou wilt not go with us, carry us not up hence." From this we learn that Moses chose rather to abide in that wilderness with his God, than go to Canaan, however rich and pleasant that country might be, without the presence of his God. "But," saith he, "if thy presence go with us, we will go." Favour us with thy presence, then we will march whichever and whatever place thou mayest command. If our journey lies through the land of Moab, or if our course runs along the borders of Amalek, with thy presence we are ready to advance. Canaan itself would be more desolate than this dreary desert, if thy presence smiled not on our faces, and shine not on our paths. This presence is the saints' portion; it makes "all things work together for their good." Every instance of Providence, every accident of life, our crosses, our sorrows, and our troubles, work in our favour. "If God be for us, who can be against us?" Jacob once cried with anguish of heart, "Me have ye bereaved of my children, Joseph is not, Simeon is not, all these things are against me." Yet old as he was, he lived long enough to see that all these things were for him. The lost having been again found, and the long absent having again been restored, his heart experienced greater joy than if they had never been removed from inside the patriarch's tent.

"All things work together for good." Whoever truly believes this sentence may overcome all his fears, and fear no dangers. Joseph's history furnishes a remarkable instance of its truth. His father sent him to his brethren. They conspired to slay him. He is rescued by Reuben, and thrown into a pit. He is taken up by Judah, and sold to the Ishmaelites. He is falsely accused by his mistress, and thrown into a prison by his master. Again, he was recommended to Pharaoh, and was made a ruler over the land of Egypt. Here many means were used, and many men employed. None of them saw God's design, yet, unknown to them, and contrary to their intentions, God made them work together with His counsel, and contribute their share to Joseph's advantage.

Not one thing, nor few things, but *all* things, are here said to work together for our good. God sometimes appears as an enemy, that He might prove our eternal friend. "Before I was afflicted," says the Psalmist, "I went astray, but now have I kept Thy word;" and here we may exclaim, "O the depth of the riches both of the wisdom and knowledge of God, how unsearchable are His judgments, and His ways past finding out." His glory is seen when He works by means, without means, but most of all when He works in opposition to means. To open the eyes of the blind was a wonderful act, but more wonderful still when clay was used as means—matter more likely to destroy than restore the sight. Awful darkness of unspeakable dread filled Abraham's soul at the very time when God was about to communicate unto him the greatest light. He struck Paul with blindness when He was about to open the eyes of his soul. "All God's ways are mercy," and "all things work together for the good of those who love Him."

Afflictions also are wonderful means whereby this truth is verified. The cross is the way to the crown. "Through much tribulation we must enter into the kingdom of God." "Thou broughtest us to the net: thou laidest affliction upon our loins: thou hast caused men to ride over our heads: we went through fire and water: and thou hast brought us to a wealthy place." The road to victory lies often along the valley of the shadow of death. The falling into the net leads to liberty, and the boasting of enemies is often a prelude to the deliverance of the saints. If this, say the enemies, is the way to life, they shall remain in it long enough: if by this means they are to raise their heads to glory, our feet shall remain on their necks yet a while. The proud man's ways shall come to the dust, and end in death. The path of the humble leads to honour, and ends in life. The journey to Canaan lay through the Red Sea, and was retarded by many provocations; on our way home we must pass through many tribulations, and have our faith exercised by many trials, yet "all work together for good to them that love God."

Afflictions are also profitable to us. The prodigal son had no thoughts of returning to his father before he had been humbled with the husk of the swine. Hagar's pride had not been subdued until she was dying of despair in the wilderness. Manasseh's heart had not been turned to the Lord, until he found himself bound with chains in the prison at Babylon. The ground which has not been ploughed and harrowed brings nothing but thorns and thistles. The heart which is not broken and contrite, can never be a pleasing sacrifice unto God.

The finest gold is purified in the fire—the best houses are built of hewn stones. We can never be vessels of honour in our Father's house unless purified in the furnace of affliction, nor be lively stones in the walls of the New Jerusalem, until our sins are cut off by the hand of God. The ungodly, "because they have no change, fear not." "Moab hath been at ease from his youth, and he hath settled on his lees, he hath not been emptied from vessel to vessel, neither hath he gone into captivity, therefore his taste remaineth in him, and his scent is not changed." O God, rather than this savour of death should rest upon us, let thy hand be upon us, to awaken us from our death-sleep, to purify us from our dross, and to cleanse us from all our sins.

It is not said that all things *shall*, but that all things *do*, work together. Not only the angels, who are our guardians, and the saints who pray for us, but that our very enemies shall minister to our profit. They have no such thoughts. This is not their aim. They meditate our destruction. It is said of that Assyrian "whom the Lord sent to punish an hypocritical nation, and to purge the wheat from the chaff, howbeit he meaneth not so, neither doth his heart think so; but, saith the Lord, though he hath no such views, yet he is only carrying on my designs." All the seeming accidents of life subserve to the same end, and centre in the same point. All tend to promote the glory of the Father, and the salvation of the children. Every reproach you suffer, every loss you sustain, every scorn that makes you blush, and every grief that makes you sad, every pain that tears your heart, and every shame that bows your head—your days of joy and days of sorrow—your plenty and your want—your health and sickness, your life and death—all combine to work together for your good. The text is a harvest of blessedness. The seed is sown. The Lord is at work. The whole creation is employed,—men and angels, friends and foes, are all engaged in promoting its growth, fencing its bounds, and ripening its produce. O God, how amazing is thy love!

If sinners purpose to extinguish the spark of fire which the Lord hath kindled in the believer's heart, their purposes shall never succeed. It is a fire from heaven, and the more the rain descends, the more it burns. It may burst into a flame, but it cannot be quenched. There are stars which shine brightest when the night is darkest. The evil intended against them is overruled for their good. Your malice is as weak to force them as your virtues are to draw them; yea, your very curses are converted into blessings. Everything works together for good to them that love God. All true believers will at last say with Joseph, "You thought evil against us, but God meant it unto good." The Philistines, envying David's growing fame, commanded him to return from the war, with the view to disgrace him. But the Lord turned their spite to David's advantage. Had he gone to battle, he would have been guilty of shedding his brethren's blood, and turning his hand against the Lord's anointed. Thus circumstances concurred to frustrate the intention of his enemies, and make *their* malice work for *his* good. The ungodly are often permitted to kill the body. They may wound unto death, but they cannot hurt the soul. God knows that the body is only a corruptible raiment, which must be soon put off, but He will preserve the soul. "Fear not them that can kill the body, but fear Him that can destroy both body and soul in hell." "Though the earth be removed, and the mountains be carried into the midst of the sea; though the waters thereof roar, and be troubled, and the mountains shake with the swelling thereof, yet there is a river which maketh glad the city of God."

Now let us inquire who are the persons for whose good God makes everything to work together—"those that love God." They are such as have been "called out of darkness into marvellous light, and translated from the kingdom of Satan into the kingdom of God's dear Son." "The love of God hath been shed abroad in their hearts." "They are a peculiar people," who shew forth the praises of Him who loved them with an everlasting love, and called them according to His purpose. These are they—the highly-favoured of the Lord—whose good is consulted in every dispensation of His providence, and in every purpose of His grace.

That all these things proceed from God is a truth everywhere acknowledged. The Psalmist saith, "I became dumb, and opened not my mouth, for it was thy doing." The patriarch Job expresses himself in the same strain, "The Lord gave, and the Lord hath taken away, blessed be the name of the Lord." Believers are not only patient under tribulations and sufferings, but grateful for them, grateful not only for God's mercies, but grateful for His judgments. As the Gospel allots many trials to the godly, so also it administers them many comforts, and strong supports. Their Great High Priest was tempted, that He might be able to succour them that are tempted. Believers know not their strength for victory, till they are tried in the day of battle. When they are surrounded with the sins which so easily beset us, they find that greater is He who is in them, than he who is in the world; as the prophet saith, Greater is He who is with you, than he who is in the world. Indeed, God's presence is always needed, but in the hour of danger it is truly sweet. This is his support under difficulties, and his solace under their crosses. Be faithful unto the end, your sufferings need your patience, God's grace will be best seen in the dark days of adversity, and God's support will be most truly felt in the hour of death. God's grace, engrafted in the heart, is a plant which neither the tares of the field nor the thorns of the roadside can break its power or choke its growth. Be strong, then, in the Lord, and in the power of His might. This will enable you to endure the heat of persecution as well as the hardness of unbelief. See that your grace is a plant which can maintain its ground against the smiles of the world, as much as against its frowns. Let not the storms of temptation put out your light, nor the flood of many waters cool the ardour of your zeal. Be stedfast in your profession, and be established in the truth. Beware lest Satan touch the white stone in your bosom, or the white robe of Christ's righteousness. Keep your conscience void of offence, and your life free from the world. "Follow the Lord wholly," in spite of all persecutions, and "live godly in Christ Jesus," in spite of all oppositions. Suffer not the sun to fade your flowers, but to ripen your fruits. Let your spark kindle into a flame, and your mustard-seed grow into a tree. Grow in grace, and press toward the mark, for the prize of your high calling, until you come to the "fulness of the stature of Christ." Let the sense of your great weakness make you draw near unto the God of all strength. Let the use of all the means of grace, like so many brooks, swell your current, till your little stream becomes a river, and your river as Jordan in the time of harvest, overflowing its banks. Let your path be as the shining light, that shineth more and more unto the perfect day. Let the blessings which have descended upon you from above, drop in the way as you go, and enrich the track you take, that you may minister grace to the hearers, and bring forth works meet for repentance, that men, seeing your good works, may glorify your Father which is in heaven. For your good, God hath engaged to make all things work together. He hath undertaken your cause, and promised

His support. Therefore invite your fellow-men to partake of your privileges, and taste of God's goodness. Being thus instruments in God's hands to arouse the careless, to awaken them that sleep, to raise up them that are fallen, you will find yourselves to be working together for your own good, and for the glory of God.

SERMON VI.

"Behold, I stand at the door and knock."—Rev. iii. 20.

BEHOLD! This expression stands in Holy Scripture as a star directing our attention to matters of weighty importance and deep significance. It is used on several occasions, and for various purposes. Sometimes to awaken our faith,—"Behold! a virgin shall conceive, and bear a son, and shall call his name Immanuel." To arouse our hopes,—"Behold! I come quickly, and my reward is with me." To excite our love,—"Behold! What manner of love the Father hath bestowed upon us that we should be called the sons of God." To alarm our fear,—"Behold! He cometh with the cloud, and every eye shall behold Him." To stir up our joy,—"Behold! I bring you good tidings of great joy." To enliven our gratitude,—"Behold! Bless ye the Lord, all ye servants of the Lord." To move our compassion,—Behold! Is there any sorrow like unto my sorrow?" and at other times, as in the text, to draw our attention to some momentous truth,—"Behold! I stand at the door and knock."

Who can contemplate this scene without feeling a thrill of joy and wonder penetrating his inward soul, seeing God, "who is of purer eyes than to behold iniquity," should seek to enter man's heart, the source of all corruption, and to dwell therein, which would be the source of all blessing and peace.

Distance seems here annihilated, and happy reconciliation effected. God and man brought under the same roof, and sit at the same table; God comes down to dwell with man, not armed with thunder, nor clothed with thick darkness, as when He descended on Mount Sinai, when the sight was so terrible that Moses said, "I exceedingly fear and quake," but "in the form of a servant made in the likeness of men." He "could break in pieces the gates of brass, and cut the bars of iron asunder." With one breath He could tear up the mountains from their roots, and burst open the portals of hell. Yet He does not come to lay waste our dwellings and level us with the ground, but stands at our doors humbly seeking for admission.

It would have been an amazing condescension to see here one of the "saints made perfect in glory," one of the prophets of old, or one of the angelic host; but it is the Prince of Peace, the King of Glory, the Lord of Hosts. He *stands* to manifest His readiness to enter in, and His patience in waiting for admission.

When we " consider the heavens which God hath made, the moon and stars which He hath ordained, at whose presence the heavens drop, and whose voice rends the rocks, yet seeing him standing at our doors, we are ready to exclaim, "What is man that thou are mindful of Him, and the Son of man that thou visitest Him." Here let us consider three things :—

    I. Who is said here to stand—God.
    II. His attitude—" I stand."
    III. His employment—" I knock."

The glorious Being who stands at the door of our hard hearts is no other than the mighty God, the creator of heaven and earth. He is before all, above all—the great and everlasting God. Neither the sun in the firmament of heaven, nor myriads of angels in glory, can in any degree approach Him who is Light of lights, and very God of very God, yet bone of our bone, and flesh of our flesh. God of His father—man of His mother—the true Melchisedec. View Him in His birth. He who inhabiteth eternity, having neither beginning nor end of days, condescends to be born in our world. The Father everlasting, an infant of a few days old—the Word unable to speak. He who upholdeth all things is himself upheld. The invisible Jehovah is seen by poor shepherds. The Lord of all disdains not to be the servant of all. At the creation man was made in the image of God, but now God appears in the form of a man. To see the sun stopping in its course, and its shadow turning back ten degrees, was an extraordinary sight, but it sinks into nothing when compared with the Sun of Righteousness coming down from heaven to earth—from the Father's bosom to the virgin's womb—from the height of glory to sojourn here below,—and from the mansions of the blessed to tabernacle amongst men. We may well then say, with one of the ancient fathers, "I shall no longer wonder at the extent of the earth, the increase or decrease of the moon, or the boundless dimensions of the sky, through which unnumbered worlds revolve, but I will wonder and adore to see God in the flesh, and the Almighty in a cradle. This is an astonishing event—the cause of great rejoicing. Rejoice, ye of the seed of Adam, for the promised seed is come. Rejoice, ye of the seed of Abraham, for "the day which he did earnestly desire to see" is come. Rejoice, ye who "sit in darkness," for "the Sun of Righteousness is risen." Rejoice, ye sinners, and be exceeding glad, for a Saviour is born into the world. Sing praises to God in the highest, for His goodwill towards men. Hear Chrysostom's melodious strain upon this joyful occasion: " O the height and depth of God's mercy, the bowels of Jesus' love. Thou art the lovely plant of the heavenly paradise. What attractions could draw thee thence? What force could draw thee out of thy Father's bosom—the palace of thy glory? Nothing but thine infinite love and infinite goodness."

Consider for what end He came. Not to increase *His* happiness, but to do *us* good, and make *us* happy. His happiness no more depends upon His creatures than the sun's bright rays are illumined by the earth's dark vapours. " Our goodness extendeth not unto Him." Before the heavens were made, He was infinitely happy. The Father rejoicing in the Son, and the Son rejoicing in the Father, and both rejoicing in the Holy Ghost. God has no more need of our service to make Him great and glorious, than the sun of the glow-worm to make it bright and genial. Were we all to perish in one day, our death, as regards God, would be only the same as the death of a thousand lepers who depend upon a rich man's alms. God created us that He might communicate His goodness, impart

His happiness, bestow His blessing, and increase the human race.

Behold, this love is not shewn unto angels, but unto men, who are the enemies of the cross of Christ, whose garments are filthy rags, whose God is their belly, and whose end is destruction; who hate Him in their thoughts, in their words, and in their actions. Truly we may say that God's ways are not like our ways; for He still waits to be gracious, and continues to knock.

II. Consider His attitude,—He stands. This implies His readiness to help, and His willingness to assist. Stephen, in the hour of his martyrdom, "saw the heavens opened, and the Son of Man standing at the right hand of God." Often He is represented as sitting on God's right hand, but when the trials of His Church are stained with the blood of martyrs, the great Captain of our salvation, having His eye fixed on the conflict, and having His sword girded upon His thigh, stands, as if ready to rush into the midst of the battle, and in the very jaws of death, to proclaim an eternal victory. Thus, in the text, He is represented as *standing*—ready to take possession of our hearts, and confer upon us the privileges of eternal life. In very moving and touching terms He solicits entrance. "O that there were such an heart in them that they would fear me, and keep my commandments, that it might be well with them, and their children for ever." To Jerusalem He saith, weeping, "How often would I have gathered thy children together, even as a hen gathereth her chickens under her wings, and ye would not." And in another place He bewails the hardness of our heart, " Ye will not come unto me, that ye might have life." Though we spurn His grace and despise His goodness, yet He still stands at those doors, that have never yet been opened to Him. He hath the power in His hand to burst open every door by force, but He hath the patience in His heart to stand and wait for admission. He could devour us in a flame of His fury, but He would rather soften us with the dew of His Spirit. Many times hath He come. Long has He been standing. "Forty years was He grieved with that generation." Slow is His anger to kindle, long is His patience to endure." But the longest day has an end. The brightest sun will ere long be set. Open your hearts to receive His message. "Kiss the Son lest He be angry," for when His wrath is kindled but a little, ye shall perish from the way." We furnish many excuses. Some have their farms and their oxen, others have their cares, and no " convenient season." The world hath its share. Sin enters in. Care and pleasure sit on the throne, evil imagination continually there do dwell, but the Saviour of men yet stands without. O my soul, answer Him whilst He calls, open whilst He knocks. Open not only the door of our lips to sing His praises, but the door of our hearts to welcome His presence. "My son, give me thine heart." Your alms will have their promised reward. Your good deeds will not lose their crown of glory. Your prayers, like incense, ascend with a sweet savour before the throne of grace, yet without the heart they are but solemn mockeries and sad delusions. As the temple sanctifies the gold, and the altar sanctifies the gift, so our heart sanctifies our prayers, consecrates our alms, and renders our good works acceptable in the sight of God. A broken and contrite heart is the most acceptable sacrifice we can ever offer. God created it, it is His workmanship, surrender it unto Him, and give Him the glory.

III. And lastly, we consider our Lord's employment,—He knocks. This He does by the ministry of His word, and this is a very powerful means. "The weapons of our warfare," saith the Apostle, " are not carnal, but mighty, through God, to the pulling down of strongholds, casting down imaginations, and every thought that exalteth itself against the knowledge of God, and bringing into captivity every thought to the obedience of Christ." When God's word "shall drop as the rain, and His speech distil as the dew, as the small rain upon the tender herb, and as the showers upon the grass," then mighty effects are instantly produced. The strongholds of unbelief totter to the ground; the hard heart is a broken sacrifice; the barren land brings forth her increase; the raging sea of persecution ceases; the swelling tide of pride ebbs; and the sea of tumultuous passion is calmed. Peace reigneth in the heart, and a thrill of joy in believing penetrates through every faculty of the soul. So mighty is the Word of God.

God knocks also by His mercies. This is a subject for angels to dwell upon, and a worthy theme for their eternal praises. Hear how they sing, and let your heart join in the chorus." The Lord is gracious, and full of compassion; slow to anger, and of great kindness; yea, His mercy is over all His works." It extends to the stars, and "reaches unto the heavens;" it pervades universal nature, and sweetens every spiritual grace; it is the penitent's prayer, "Lord have mercy upon me;" it is the saint's song, "for thy mercy endureth for ever."

He knocks by afflictions. These are God's messengers. Their solicitations are earnest, close, and pressing. By them we are earnestly invited to come to God, and by them God seeks to come to us. They brought Naaman to the prophet in Israel, and made the lepers come to Christ. Afflictions made the prodigal remember his father's house, and prevented the apostle to be " lifted up above measure." By them the wicked often cease from troubling, and believers are drawn nearer to God. Ephraim, unaccustomed to the yoke, lifts up his heel against heaven; Israel, smitten and slain, " returned and inquired after God; David's sweetest songs were composed in David's greatest troubles; " our light affliction, which is but for a moment, worketh for us a far more exceeding and eternal weight of glory."

He knocks by His judgments. The prophet exclaims, " in the way of thy judgments have we waited for thee; in trouble have we visited thee; we poured forth a prayer, when thy chastening was upon us." Often He strikes at our neighbour's door, warning us, " except ye repent ye shall likewise perish." The clouds, which are gathering at a distance may soon break over our heads. Happy is the man who learns from the corrections of others, how to correct himself. When God's judgments are upon the earth, may the inhabitants learn righteousness.

He knocks by the law. This shows sin in its true nature and real features. It was originally given amongst thunder and lightning. It still strikes with irresistible power, and cuts its way with awful force. It reveals God's wrath, and declares God's justice. The apostle saith, "I was alive without the law once"—that is, I had a good opinion of the state of my soul, and saw myself in no danger; but when the law, in all its convincing power, reached my soul, "I died," all my hopes vanished, all my high thoughts withered, and all my previous notions died. You are lost, you perish, and in this state you will also die, and remain for ever, as long as you keep Jesus Christ out of your heart, and refuse Him admission when He knocks.

He also knocks by the Gospel. This sets forth our blessed Saviour as the only means of our salvation—it exhibits the riches of His grace, the fulness of His redemption, and the sweetness of His love. To the weary He offers rest—the heavy-laden He will refresh. The naked He will clothe, the hungry He will feed. Sight He will give to the blind, and upon the poor He will pour the riches of His grace. If you refuse, you make Him weep; if you harden your hearts, you grieve His Spirit. The greatest misery He can remove, and the greatest compassion He is ready to shew.

Some may say, " we can do nothing; and why should we be required to perform that which is not in our power to do?" It would be well if this was really believed. This is the great obstacle in the way of happiness. As long as we think that we have some strength of our own, we will not go to God for help. If we have lost the power of obeying, still God hath not lost His authority to demand. A sum of money lent, and afterwards lost, would not invalidate the claim. So we received and lost all in Adam; and though having lost the power to obey, yet God still claims the authority to demand, and nothing is impossible with God. By His word He heals the broken and contrite heart; and by His Spirit He now quickens souls dead in trespasses and sins. May this be "the hour in which the dead among you shall hear the voice of the Son of God, and live." May His voice reach you, as it reached Lazarus in the grave, saying, "Come forth;" and may His Holy Spirit quicken your life and sanctify your souls. Some may plant, and others may water; but it is God alone who can give the increase.

In conclusion, consider for what purpose, and to whom, you are to open your hearts. It is to Him who gave your lives, and shed His blood to save your souls. As the prophet prayed for his servant, that the Lord God would open his eyes, so it is my earnest petition that God should open your hearts. Receive Christ, and reserve no room for self and sin. If you open to Him, you shall have God and His fulness. You shall have on earth the riches of His grace, and in heaven an eternal weight of glory. He will be with you here. He will support you in death; and, oh! on that awful day, when heaven and earth shall pass away, and the whole system of the universe be dashed to thousand atoms, then, yea, then He will own you. Open to Him now, and this blessedness you will realize hereafter, through Jesus Christ our Lord. Amen.

SERMON VII.

◆

"Yet Michael the archangel, when contending with the devil, (he disputed about the body of Moses), durst not bring against him a railing accusation, but said, The Lord rebuke thee."—JUDE 9.

THE apostle, after uttering his complaints against those filthy dreamers who despised dominion, and spake evil of dignities—great men whom God had raised in His Church—proceeds to compare their conduct towards men with the conduct of the archangel towards the devil. If Michael, who was by nature so excellent, and by office so exalted, when he was disputing with the devil, an evil and impious spirit, treats him with such leniency, how dare they, who are such mean, wretched creatures, treat with insolence and contempt persons placed in eminent stations, and invested with sovereign power? If the archangel, when engaged in a good cause, refrained from bringing any charges against the very devil himself, how dare they vent their rage, and curse men far superior and better than themselves? The sum of the whole is this, if an angel of such worth and dignity refrained from bringing any railing accusation against the worst of beings, how dare bad men presume to revile those whom God hath put in authority either in Church or State. Having thus shewn the apostles' mode of arguing, I proceed to consider the words more particularly, and to draw therefrom such words of instruction, as may, under the guidance of Divine grace, not only inform your understandings, but improve your hearts. The word "Michael," means, who is like unto God? The learned differ in their opinions touching this exalted being. Some suppose him to be the second person in the ever-blessed Trinity. Others maintain that he is a created being of the highest order, whose station is near the throne of God, ready to receive and excute His maker's supreme commands. This supposition is strongly confirmed by a passage in the prophecy of Daniel, where he is styled "one of the chief princes." As Beelzebub is called the chief of the devils, so Michael is supposed to be the chief of the angels. The word "devil" signifies an accuser or slanderer. His first act after his fall was falsehood, and even denying that death would be the fruit of disobedience, and stating that God was afraid that our first parents should taste of the tree, lest they should become like unto Him, "for He doth know that in the day ye eat thereof, then your eyes shall be opened, and ye shall be as gods, knowing good and evil."

This work he still persists to do. Sometimes he slanders God's justice, insinuating that He will never inflict the punishment denounced against sin in His holy law. At other times he represents God as utterly devoid of mercy, and with cunning malignity, softened and concealed under the cloak of sympathy, suggests, even to the penitent, that their sins are greater than can be forgiven. He employs every stratagem which falsehood, envy, and malice can effect, and uses every art which wickedness, treachery, and jealousy can devise, for cutting off those whom God only intended to humble, and frustrate God's design in their salvation. He is also called in the Book of Revelation, the accuser of the brethren, who accuseth them before God day and night. He withstood Joshua the high-priest, standing before the angel. He charged Job with the love of self-interest, and not with the love of God, insinuating that if his wishes were once removed, his love would soon grow cold, and his service would soon cease. He makes every effort to condemn those whom the Lord hath acquitted. But the venom which he throws at them recoils upon himself, and the stratagems he employs for their destruction are overruled for their protection. With fearful audacity, he dares accuse the brethren before Him who sees through his falsehood, baseness, and injustice, and who will hereafter judge the accuser and pity the accused. He excites jealousy amongst men, and envy between brethren. By him Elijah is accused of troubling Israel, and our Saviour of being an enemy to Cæsar. Resist, then, the devil, and trust in the Lord, "for He shall bring forth your righteousness as the light, and your judgment as noon day. Christ is beyond his reach; but those who resemble Him the most, Satan tries to ensnare on their way home, and however much he succeeds, he can never prevent them reaching their journey's end.

He is also a deceiver, and often leads man to deceive himself. Every kind of deceit is both hateful and dangerous, but self-deceit should be most dreaded. "Be ye doers of the work, and not hearers only, deceiving your ownselves." The Syrians imagined they were going to Dathan, whilst they were actually marching towards Samaria. There are still thousands imagining themselves going along the narrow path to heaven, whilst they are on the broad road to destruction. They use every means to hide all sins in themselves; and in others, whom they hate, they delight to mark what is done amiss.

From the conduct of Michael, as shewn on this occasion, we should learn that the higher we are exalted the more humble we should be. No creature is higher than the archangel, and yet no creature is so low. None so vile as the devil, and yet none so proud. Humility is the ornament and the glory of the angels, but pride is the disgrace and deformity of devils, and if heaven would not retain a proud angel, it will never receive a proud soul. The more numerous are the gifts you receive, the greater should be the depth of your humility, for all you have you received from God; pride not yourselves upon the gifts, but give glory to the Giver—of this He is jealous, and declares that His glory He will not give to others, nor His praise to graven images. "Watch and pray," lest your pride be your destruction, and your glory end in shame.

From the archangel's contending with the devil about the body of Moses, we may learn that there is a contest between good and bad spirits concerning both temporal and spiritual matters. Good angels contend about the safety of the saints in this world, and, like a troop of armed soldiers, " encamp round about them to deliver them." They keep them in their ways, and " bear them in their hands, lest at any time they dash their foot against a stone." They encamped around Elisha when he was surrounded by his enemies. And when "the Lord opened the eyes of the young man," he beheld "the mountain full of horses and chariots, round about Elisha." When Daniel had been cast into the lions' den, an angel closed the lions' mouths. When Jezebel sought Elijah's life, angels supplied his wants and cheered his solitude. But, on the other hand, Satan, with a host of evil spirits, goes about "seeking to devour" God's people, and hurl them to eternal destruction. His whole aim is to corrupt men's hearts, and to ruin their souls. He is their great enemy. It is his greatest pleasure to undermine their character, and injure their reputation. He stirred up Jannes and Jambres to withstand Moses. He became a lying spirit in the mouth of Baal's prophets. He sowed tares in that field where good seed had been sown. He hindered Paul on his journeys, and cast saints into prison. In every age, and in every place, this contest between Christ and the devil—between holiness and sin—is going on. Angels are engaged in the conflict, and men are interested in the issue. With man it is often an inward struggle, with angels a continual contest; good angels carolled the Messiah's birth, when evil spirits sought to slay Him in his infancy. The devil tempted

Jesus in the wilderness, but angels came and ministered to His wants. They desire to look into the mysteries of the Gospel, and rejoice in the conversion of one sinner. The contest which is fiercely waged between these armies of the sky, exists also between the graces of the one and the crimes of the other, virtue and vice are contrary to each other, and sin and holiness can never co-exist—sin hates holiness, and holiness cannot endure sin. Sin is as loathsome to grace, as grace is hateful to sin. It is "the flesh lusting against the spirit, and the spirit against the flesh, and they are contrary the one to the other."

Believers may hence learn that as long as they continue holy, they can expect no rest. In the world they shall have tribulation. They must bear with insults, slander, and persecution; they must not be discouraged at the reproaches of men, nor be dismayed at the attacks of Satan;—neither is a bad symptom. It was the treatment which angels received, and the very same reception was given unto the Son of God. Let them alone; their scoff is no scandal, and Satan's buffettings are no signs of God's hatred. When he sallies forth in his great strength against us, the Archangel will enter into the contest, and the great Captain of our salvation will stand up in our defence. "If God be for us, who can be against us?" The heavenly hosts rank on our side, and their service they have always rendered unto the children of God. "Take heed that ye despise not one of these little ones, for I say unto you, that in heaven their angels do always behold the face of my Father who is in heaven." These may be little in faith, little in their own esteem, and little in the eyes of the world, yet they are great in the sight of the angels of God. They see in them the heirs of salvation, and esteem it all honour to render them any service, for, "are they not all ministering spirits, sent forth to minister for them?" It is not said *they were*, but *they are*, even now encamping around God's people, as faithful sentinels, to guard their charge, and continue their watch till all dangers finally cease, and until they safely reach their home.

Michael disputed about the body of Moses. The only account recorded of Moses' burial is found in Deut. xxxiv. 6, where it is said, "He buried him in a valley, in the land of Moab; but no man knoweth of the sepulchre unto this day." From this passage it is evident that the Lord buried him. Whether He commanded the angels to dig his grave, or the earth to open its mouth to receive his body, is not known; yet it is certain that he was buried; and it is supposed that the devil was desirous to be present, that he might see where the corpse was deposited, in order that the Israelites might be induced to resort to the spot, and make him an object of idolatry; but Michael withstood him, and frustrated his intentions. Hence we may learn that the devil's sole object is to lead men astray, in the paths of sin. As it is our Lord's design to promote our growth in grace, so is it Satan's aim to ruin our souls, and make us more like unto himself. His object in the case of Job was to lead him to impatience and distrust. He was not so much for depriving him of his wealth, as he was for sifting his grace. "Satan," saith Christ to Peter, "hath desired to have you, that he might sift you as wheat; but I have prayed for thee, that thy faith fail not." He aims at the Christian's deeds more than at his person or possessions. He employs every artifice to check the Christian's growth in grace, and nothing is so sweet to him as the death of souls. As the best of men are the objects of his attacks, so the best thing they have—even their graces and their souls—are the objects of his gain.

When Michael disputed with the devil about the body of Moses, he durst not bring a railing accusation against him. When by accident or temptation we are thrown in the devil's way, it is yet a great blessing to be kept from sin. Michael contends with the devil, yet he is still holy. Our Saviour was tempted by him in the wilderness, but He remained still undefiled. The strength of God's grace is made more manifest when you remain untainted amongst corruption, than when you shun the society of the wicked. It is a great blessing if you can mix with the world, and yet not being *of* the world. To do this effectually, first examine your own faults, and inspect your own heart. The nearest enemy is the worst enemy—your sins lie in your bosom. Let them also be the most odious in your sight. May also God's love influence your hearts, for as "love thinketh no evil," so truly it speaketh no evil. Envy and malice invent mischief; but "love covers a multitude of sins." Entreat the Lord "to set a watch over your mouth," and resolve, with David, "not to offend with your tongue." "Recompense to no man evil for evil," but "bless, and curse not." Let the door of your lips be so sealed that it cannot be open by any provocation; and let your neighbour's name be regarded as your own. If you permit his name to be slandered in your presence, your reputation will share the same fate, for with "what measure ye mete, it shall be measured to you again."

"He durst not." From this expression we may learn that the grace of God is not only a restraint from sin, but a strong defence against sin. As long as you fear God, you need not heed man. Sanctify the Lord wholly in your hearts, and He will be your tower of defence in the day of evil. Choose rather to suffer every ridicule for your sanctity, than to be condemned for your sin. "The fear of the Lord is to hate evil," and this fear constrains us not only to abstain from outward sin, but inwardly to hate sin. It will not only bind our hands, but it will also change our hearts. The fear of man may make us hide our sins, but the fear of God makes us to loathe them. They who tremble at God's word, shall ever smart under God's rod. Godly fear is the spring, whence, through God's grace, issues the Christian's hope. Noah, through fear, built the ark, and rested in the days of trouble. A railing accusation is a sin strictly forbidden in the word of God, and it was severely punished in the time of the prophet Elisha, when "there came two bears out of the wood and tore forty and two children in Bethel." By railing at others we injure our ownselves. Railing is a deadly poison, which produces fatal mortification, causing division and hatred amongst even brethren—who, before the tale-bearer came in, dwelt together in peace and unity. The railer sins against God, injures his neighbour, and is a sad enemy to himself. Whilst he wounds others, he poisons his own soul; and in blasting his neighbour's fame, he exposes his own folly.

Solomon saith, that "he who uttereth slander is a fool," and seems utterly inconsistent with the spirit of true religion. "If any among you seems to be religious, and bridleth not his tongue but deceiveth his own heart, that man's religion is vain." "The poison of asps is under his lips, and with his tongue he cuts as with a sharp razor."

It is probable that Satan roared, his mouth being full of blasphemies, for it is said, that "he opened his mouth in blasphemy against God, to blaspheme His name, and His tabernacle, and them who dwelt in heaven." But Michael was of another spirit. He avenged not himself, but left it to Him to whom it belonged. "Vengeance is mine, and I will repay it, saith the Lord." This should teach us patience and meekness under all provocations. "For even hereunto we are called; because Christ also suffered for us, leaving us an example, that we may follow His steps, who did no sin, neither was guile found in His mouth; who, when He was reviled, reviled not again; when He suffered, He threatened not, but committed himself to Him who judgeth righteously." Learn hence, meekness, for Jesus does not require of you to learn to create a world, to walk on the sea, to feed thousands with a few loaves and fishes, to cleanse the lepers, to give sight to the blind, to hush the wind, to heal diseases, or to cast out devils, but to learn meekness. "Learn of me," saith He, "for I am meek and lowly in heart." He was "the Lamb of God," so ought we to be—lambs, not lions; sheep, not wolves. If we "bite and devour one another, we should take heed that we should not consume one another."

Michael delivered Satan into the hands of God, that He might rebuke him; and his conduct conformed with the spirit of the Scripture, which enjoins us not to say, "I will recompense evil; I will do unto him as he hath done unto me;" but to "wait on the Lord, and He will save us." Pray for thine enemy, and forgive thy brother." Remember our Saviour's prayer on the cross, "Father, forgive them, for they know not what they do." Return good for evil, and love them that hate you. Weary them with your patience, and follow the example of your God.

SERMON VIII.

"As new born babes, desire the sincere milk of the word, that ye may grow thereby."—1 PETER ii. 2.

THIS Scripture contains an affectionate address to believing Jews, entreating them to grow in faith, and give due attention to God's Word, as the means whereby that growth is promoted. The apostle exhorts them to hunger and thirst for that Word of God, which is the food and nourishment of the soul, in the same manner as babes cry for their mother's breast, whose milk feeds and nourishes them. The words allude to two kinds of birth, one earthly and natural, implying that birth from our first parents, through whom, original sin, like the poison of an asp, hath defiled the whole human race: the other is heavenly and spiritual, implying that birth which is of God, through whom grace and holiness nourish and sanctify our souls. In this last birth, God is our Father to beget us, the

Church is our mother to give us birth. The Word of God is the means whereby we are begotten; the ministers of the Gospel are they who feed us, and the Gospel itself is that breast which yields nourishment to our souls. We shall here state—

I. The qualification required of those who wish to grow in grace, "They must be as new born babes."
II. The first act of the mind in babes, "They desire."
III. What are we to desire, "The milk of the word."
IV. What kind of milk, "The *sincere* milk of the word."
V. The object in view for desiring this milk of the word, "That we may grow thereby."

I. We know that babes are innocent, simple, and harmless. This also should be the character of all who would be instructed in the Word of God, or be enlightened and comforted by the preaching of the Gospel. We must be converted, and become as little children, before we can ever enter into the kingdom of God. They who would have the Lord Jesus to reveal unto them His will, must be cleansed from all iniquity and sin. For as Satan will not dwell in a house where true religion reigns, so the Spirit of God will not long dwell in any habitation which is not swept, cleansed, and garnished. As long as we do not desire new hearts, we cannot expect new blessings, our preaching and your hearing will be all in vain, unless the veil of sin be removed, and the light of the Gospel shine in our hearts. If you wish that the Lord would bless your hearing, and give success to our preaching, you must cast off the dregs of sin which sour your souls, and the rust of sin which corrupts your heart, lest, instead of a blessing, you receive a curse, and lest the Word of God, which should be a savour of life unto life, should be the savour of death unto death. As the unbelief of the Jews prevented Christ from working many miracles among them, so the bosom sins of your hearts quench His Spirit, and close, as it were, His mouth. The prophet's counsel was "to break up the fallow ground, and not to sow among thorns," that is, among those worldly cares that spring up and choke the plants of instruction and truth. To see the diligence of the husbandman, and perceive the carelessness of the Christian, causes a good man to be grieved in his inmost soul. He may see many going up to the house of God with an evil spirit in their hearts, and many coming out with the curse of God upon their heads. Many spend more time to adorn their bodies, to appear before men, than they employ in prayer to sanctify their souls, and prepare to come before God. Abhor these sinful practices, and long to be, not only as little children, but as little babes, having new hearts, new members, new desires, and a new life ingrafted in your souls. Abstain not only from one sin, but from all appearance of evil, so as to become other men, or new creatures in Christ Jesus. If you be attentive hearers, put away from you your lusts and passions, and come as little children to hear the Word of God. And if you would hear profitably, be simple as little children, free from all prejudices, and separated from all sin. Be renewed in the spirit of your minds, and, like new born babes, desire the sincere milk of the Word, that ye may grow thereby.

II. The first act of the mind in babes—to desire. We are not to be like wavering children, " tossed to and fro, and carried about with every wind of doctrine," neither are we to be children in knowledge and understanding. "Brethren," saith the apostle, "be not children in understanding, howbeit, in malice be ye children, but in understanding be ye men." Neither, then, in understanding nor knowledge are we to be children, but as new born babes we are to desire the sincere milk of the Word. "Blessed are they who do hunger and thirst after righteousness, for they shall be filled." God satisfieth the hungry with good things, and the rich He sends empty away. When we are fervent in spirit, and feel an actual desire and thirst after God's Word, we may certainly conclude that we have a new life and a new spirit in us, and that every spark of religion is not utterly gone out, and that we are not wholly dead. It would be the same thing to desire the dead to quit their graves, as to see those dead in trespasses and sin—desiring not the Word of truth—leave their sins and save their souls. Many imagine the Word can give life of itself, and hence seek not the Spirit of God, who creates the new birth and nourishes the new souls. They complain of the length of the service, and are best pleased with the shortest prayer, forgetting the sentiments of those saints who "delighted in the law of the Lord, and in His law meditated day and night," who "departed not from the temple, but served God with fastings and prayers, night and day;" they have no relish for God's Word, and evince no anxiety for the salvation of their own souls. As new born babes cry for the mother's breast as soon as they are born, so should Christians, as soon as they hear of a new and another life, hunger and thirst after the milk of the Word. A child who was not fed could not live for three days, much less can our faith subsist without being fed and nourished by the bread of life. Our Lord commanded that something should be given to eat to Jairus' daughter, as soon as He had raised her from the dead, intimating that in vain we be revived by God's finger unless we are fed by the Word of His grace. When God quickens us by His Spirit, and we experience His grace implanted in our hearts, we should water it, lest it be scorched up like the seed which fell on the rocky ground, and withered away. We deem it a great miracle that Elijah lived forty days without food, but it is a matter of greater astonishment that souls should exist forty years without tasting of the bread of life. As our Lord was sent for to heal the ruler's daughter when she was at the point of death, so many will not seek the prayers of God's ministers until they are arrested by the hand of death. They wish to die the death of the righteous, though they have lived the lives of the wicked; they now seek for repentance whose offers they had before despised; they delay building the ark until they are overtaken with the deluge. Lot tarried in Sodom, until, in a manner, the angels forced him to depart; and in truth, if God does not pluck us as brands out of the burning fire by His grace, and by His Spirit remove the veil of ignorance and darkness from our souls, none can be saved. Wherefore, if ye have been planted in the true faith, see that ye are also watered, for the best gifts will soon decay if they be not moistened by the dew of heaven. As children, eager for food, are deaf to all excuses until they are satisfied, so, in like manner, it is not enough for you to desire the the Word, but you should be earnest and importunate in your prayers, that it should be ingrafted in your hearts that ye may grow thereby. "The word of Christ should dwell in us richly." It is not enough that it should remain for a while, and then to depart, but it must abide daily and continually in our hearts. It should be the food of our souls, morning, noon, and night. Though the ground may be good, yet it still needs the former and the latter rain, before it can ever bring forth much fruit. Some imagine that one shower, one sermon, or one prayer, will abundantly water their souls. Not so, brethren, ye must strive to enter in at the strait gate. As new born babes, ye must desire the sincere milk of the Word, immediately, without delay; incessantly, without weariness; cheerfully, without murmuring; constantly, without ceasing; and perseveringly, unto the end.

III. What we are to desire—the milk of the Word—that is, our food and sustenance in

Christ Jesus. For this we are to labour more than for any other food. Thus our Saviour commands. "Labour not," saith He, "for the meat which perisheth: but for that meat which endureth unto everlasting life." And although "the Word of God endureth for ever," and is the "incorruptible seed" which preserves from famine and death, yet we desire many things before it. There is a carnal desire which wars against the soul—there is a desire of money, which is the root of all evil. There is a desire of retaliation, which springs from the spirit of revenge, and a desire of praise, which springs from pride; but few have the real desire for the sincere Word of truth. Among the many blessings wherewith the land of Canaan abounded, the chief was, "that it flowed with milk and honey;" but the Word of God abounds with far greater treasures, bears higher titles, and holds out far greater promises. It is a "lamp to guide our feet, and a light unto our path." It is a medicine to heal our wounds, and a bridle to check our pride. It is a milk to nourish, and a wine to cheer. It is a sword to defend us on our journey home, and a key to open to us the gate of heaven. And as Elisha said unto Naaman concerning Jordan, "Wash in it and be clean," so may we say to all respecting the Word of God, "Feed on it, and live for ever." It is the golden chain which brings God and man together. It gives hope to the cast down, and imparts strength to the weary. It refreshes the heavy-laden, and gives eternal life to all believers. It speaks peace to the conscience. It gladdens the heart, it consoles the spirit, and gives inexpressible joy in believing. Despise not the Word of God, for by it you now live, and by it you will be judged in the last day.

IV. Its nature and quality. It is called the "*sincere* milk of the word." It is as milk in its natural state—not mixed with any error, nor soured by any prejudice. And as our Saviour admonishes us "*how* we hear," so the apostle warns us "to take heed *what* we hear." For as there is a doctrine full of purity and truth, so also there is a doctrine full of leaven and malice. There is a communication which ministers grace to the hearers, and there is a communication that corrupts good manners. There is a word that edifies, and there is a word that eats like a canker. There is a teaching of God, and there are doctrines of devils. And as it was once said, "There is death in the pot," so it may be also said, there is death in the food; and for this reason, we are so often enjoined in Scripture to " beware of false prophets, who come to us in sheep's clothing, but inwardly not better than ravening wolves;" and not to "believe every spirit, but that we try the spirits, whether they be of God." Many, like the prodigal son, feed upon the husks of the swine: hear they do, but to no good: driven about by many winds of doctrine, but neither grow in grace nor increase in knowledge. Truth can have no fellowship with error. Take heed lest unscriptural doctrines corrupt your heart, and ruin your souls. To pretend to be worshipping God at church in the morning, and carousing at the public-house in the evening, cannot less than produce a canker in your bosom which must end in your death.

V. And last place. We will consider the end in view for thus desiring the sincere milk of the Word,—that we may grow thereby. The design, then, is, that we may grow in grace, grow in faith, and grow in righteousness.

Believers are called "the trees of righteousness," intimating that they grow. They are also called faithful servants, who trade with their Lord's talents, that they may receive their own with usury. We are not always to be children, but we must henceforth "increase in stature, till we come to the fulness of Christ. We should walk forward in the path of duty, until we come to the full fruition of God. We must advance from grace to grace. We must not only go and hear the Word of God, but we must needs profit by our hearing. We should be more zealous, more faithful, and more active for the truth, than we have been in the past. We must be more holy, more fervent, and more diligent in religion in the future. It is to be feared that many who have long ago heard the Word, are yet still of little faith, of little love, of little patience, and of little humility, that they have not yet seen Christ. Nay, several are still as dishonest towards their neighbours, as they are negligent in the service of God, as proud in their hearts, as hypocritical at their church, and as sinful at their home, as they have ever been. The reason is, they hear the Word, but they do not grow thereby. But be assured, brethren, that it would have been better for you not to have heard, than not to profit thereby. If the servant who hid his talent in the ground, was cast into outer darkness, of what punishment shall they be counted worthy, who spend their talents upon their own pleasure? We should take heed what we hear, lest we receive the grace of God in vain. We should not only hear, read, mark, and learn, but inwardly digest it, that we may grow thereby. If ye are desirous of a blessing on the Word of God, be sure to look up unto the Lord, and direct your prayer unto Him, to preserve you in the spiritual conflict in which you are about to engage. Separate yourselves from sinners whilst you seek for light to walk the narrow road; and when circumstances call you into their society, let your conversation resemble that of the two disciples. You may then hope that Jesus may be in your company. Do not deem it sufficient to be found within the walls of the church, but seek also to see Jesus there, that the word of salvation may effectually come to your heart. Beware, lest, while " ye tread His courts," you bring vain oblations—an incense which is an abomination unto the Lord. Take heed that the sacred flame which hath been kindled in your heart be not put out by your sin, but let your prayer be a real burnt-offering unto the Lord—a service acceptable in His sight, improve your talents. Be ye doers of the Word, that may you grow in grace, and may your graces be multiplied through Jesus Christ our Lord.

SUBSCRIBERS' NAMES.

H. R. H. P. W., 6 copies.
The Right Rev. the Lord Bishop of St Asaph, 6 copies.
The Right Hon. the Earl of Shaftesbury, 4 copies.
The Right Hon. Lord Dynevor, 4 copies.
The Right Rev. the Lord Bishop of St David's, 4 copies.
The Right Rev. the Lord Bishop of Bangor, 2 copies.
The Right Hon. Lord Boston, 4 copies.
The Right Hon. Lord Ebury, 4 copies.
The Right Hon. Lord Richard Grosvenor, 4 copies.
The Right Hon. the Earl of Powis, 4 copies.
The Right Hon. Lord Llanover (late), 2 copies.
The Right Hon. the Countess of Lisburne, 2 copies.
The Right Hon. Earl Vane, 4 copies.
The Hon. Lady Willoughby De Broke, 3 copies.

Adami, John George, Esq., Albion Hotel, Manchester.
Ainger, Rev. Dr, Principal of St Bees College.

Andrews, Rev. E., Vicar of Llandyfeilog, Carmarthen.
Ashbury, James, Esq., 9 Sussex Place, Hyde Park Gardens.

Barbour, R., Esq., Bolesworth Castle, Tattenhall, 4 copies.
Barnard, Mrs C., Brocklesby Rectory, Ulceby.
Barnes, Thomas, Esq., M.P., Quinta, Chirk, 2 copies.
Bazley, Thomas, Esq., M.P., 5 St James Square, 2 copies.
Bass, Messrs & Co., Burton-on-Trent.
Bellingham, William, Esq., Wrexham.
Bevan, Mr (Caradawc y Fenni), Abergavenny.
Biddulph, Col. R. Myddleton, M.P., Chirk Castle, 2 copies.
Birch, Mr T. E., Chemist, Mold.
Blake, T. Jex, Esq., Brighton, 2 copies.
Blackie & Sons, Messrs, 44 Paternoster Row, E.C.
Blackwall, J., Esq., Hendre House, Llanrwst.
Boulger, Rev. J. Pennant, Llanrwst.
Bowker, William, Esq., Mayor, Manchester.
Brassey, Thos., Esq., Westminster, S.W., 2 copies.
Brereton, Mr (Andreas o Fôn), Mold.
Bright, John, Esq., M.P., Rochdale.
Bromley, N., Esq., High Street, Manchester.
Bruce, Right Hon. H. Austin, M.P., 2 copies.
Buddicom, W. B., Esq., Pembedw Hall, Mold.
Burgess, Mrs, Chesworth, 6 Trafford Road, Old Trafford, Manchester.
Buxton, C., Esq., Fox-warren, Cobham, 2 copies.

SUBSCRIBERS' NAMES.

Cadman, Mrs, Handsworth Grange, Sheffield, 2 copies.
Carne, Dr Nichol, St Donat's Castle, Cowbridge, 2 copies.
Castree, Josiah, Esq., College Green, Gloucester.
Charles, Rev. D., Abercarn, Newport, Mon.
Conway, Wm., Esq., 1 Chapel Walks, Manchester.
Clemense, Captain, Parc-Arthur, Mold, 2 copies.
Creed, J., Esq., Whiddon House, Newton Abbot, 2 copies.
Creed, W., Esq., Solicitor, Newton Abbot.

Dalton, Rev. W. H., Lloyd's House, Wolverhampton, 3 copies.
Darby, C., Esq., Brymbo, Wrexham, 2 copies.
Dargue, Mr T., 62 Benshaw Street, Liverpool.
Davies, D., Esq., Llandinam, 4 copies.
Davies, J. C., Esq., M.D., Holywell.
Davies, Miss, Penmaen-Dovey, Machynlleth, 2 copies.
Davies, Rev. W., Vicarage, Llanwonno, Pontypridd.
Davies, Thomas, Esq., Towy Villa, Llandeilo.
Davies, Rev. W. Smith, Tonge, Middleton, Manchester.
Davies, Rev. W., Penydarren, Merthyr Tydvil.
Davies, Mr, St David's Church, Liverpool.
Davies, Henry, Esq., Harley Lodge, Cheltenham.
Davies, Richard, Esq., Penarth, Conway, 2 copies.
Davies, Rev. Octavius, Aberystwyth.
Davies, Mr T. Jones, George Town, Merthyr-Tydvil.
Davies, Captain Francis, Pershore, 2 copies.
Davies, James, Esq., Solicitor, Hereford.

Davies, Rev. D., Castle Rectory, Welshpool, 2 copies.
Davies, Rev. W., Llangadeyrne, Carmarthen.
Davies, Rev. Thomas, M.A., Vicar of Dihewyd and Llanerchaeron, Cardiganshire.
Davies, Mr, Schoolmaster, Llanddarog-Kidwelly.
Davies, David, Esq., Castle Green, Cardigan.
Davies, W., Esq., (Gwilym Teilo), F.G.H.S., Llandeilo.
Dyos, Miss Heyward, Garthderwen House, Welshpool.
Dixon, Rev. Alexander, Higham Ferrers, Northants, 2 copies.
Dobie, Miss, Gyleburn, Lockerbie.
Drummond, Rev. Spencer R., St John's, Brighton.
Dodd, Robert, Esq., East-Gate, Chester, 2 copies.
Douglas, J. K., Esq., Bangor.

Edmunds, Rev. W., Lampeter.
Edwards, Rev. H. T., Vicarage, Aberdare.
Edwards, Rev. Edward, Eglwysfach, Aberystwyth.
Edwards, Rev. D. E., Pentre Broughton, Wrexham.
Edwards, Charles, Esq., M.P., Dolserau, Dolgelly, 2 copies.
Edwards, Rev. J., Cefnygwyn, Talicsin, Shrewsbury, 2 copies.
Ellerton, William, Esq., Tranmere, Birkenhead.
Erskine, The Dowager Lady, Conway House, Torquay, 2 copies.
Evans, Rev. Daniel, L.T.D., Llansantffread-ar-Ogwr, Bridgend.
Evans, Rev. E., Vicar of Pyle, Bridgend.
Evans, Rev. D., Vicarage, Bala.

Evans, Captain, Walwen, Holywell.
Evans, Rev. W., Incumbent of Rhymney.
Evans, Mr, National School, Gwernafield, Mold.
Evans & Co., Messrs, Eastgate Buildings, Chester.
Evans, Rev. Lewis, B.A., Principal of Ystradmeurig School, 4 copies.
Evans, Rev. J. (Eigrad) Talybont, *via* Shrewsbury.
Evans, John S. H., Esq., Fron Don, Rhyl.
Evans, Rev. Evan T., Tredegar.
Evans, Rev. Edward, Dowlais, Merthyr Tydvil.
Evans, Rev. J. B., Vicarage, St Hermon, Rhayadar.
Everett, Mr R. P., Draper, Mold.
Ewing, Charles, Esq., Golden Grove, Chester.

Faithfull, Mrs, Llanwenarth Rectory, Abergavenny, 4 copies.
Farbridge, R. J., Esq., Greenway, Cheltenham.
Farish, James, Esq., 26 Upper Hamilton Terrace, N.W., 2 copies.
Farmer, George, Esq., Surveyor, Montgomery.
Ffoulkes, Mr I., 41 Peter Lane, Liverpool, 2 copies.
Ffoulkes, Mr, 3 Alder Street, Liverpool.
Francis, W., Esq., Holway House, Holywell.
Francis, Mr, Piccadilly, Manchester.
Francis, John, Esq., Town Hall, Manchester.
Friend, A.
Frimstone, Mr, Friday Street, Manchester.
Frodsham, Frederick, Esq., Solicitor, Liverpool, 2 copies.

Games, Dr, Highfield Street, Liverpool.

Gee, Mr, Publisher, Denbigh.
Geldart, Thomas, Esq., 51 Piccadilly, Manchester.
Gladstone, Robertson, Esq., Court Hay, Liverpool, 2 copies.
Glynne, Rev. H., R. D., Hawarden Rectory, 2 copies.
Gower, Rev. J., Home Missionary, Tondû, Bridgend.
Green, Francis, Esq., Solicitor, Carmarthen.
Griffith, Rev. A., Vicar of Llanelly, Abergavenny, 2 copies.
Griffith, Mr John, Eastgate Street, Chester.
Griffith, Rev. J., M.A., Vicarage, Merthyr Tydvil.
Griffith, Miss Conway, Garreglwyd, Holyhead, 2 copies.
Griffith, Thomas Lloyd, Esq., Tunbridge Wells.
Griffith, Rev. D., Resolven Vicarage, Neath.
Griffith, Rev. John, B.D., Vicar of Llandeilo.
Gwyn, Howell, Esq., Dyffryn, Neath, 2 copies.
Guest, Edwin, Esq., LL.D., F.R.S., Gonville and Caius, Cambridge, 2 copies.

Hall, Thomas, Esq., 6 Commercial Street, London.
Hanmer, Sir John, M.P., Hanmer Hall, Shrewsbury, 4 copies.
Harris, Rev. J. J., Amlwch.
Havard, Rev. L., Roman Catholic Church, Brecon.
Haworth, R., Esq., High Street, Manchester.
Hengoed, Mr, Llangadeyrne, Kidwelly.
Herbert, Colonel Hon. P. E., M.P., Berkley Square, 2 copies.
Herbert, Rev. Edward, Rector of Llandyfrydog, Anglesey, 2 copies.

SUBSCRIBERS' NAMES. 259

Holland, Rev. T. A., Rector of Poynings, Hurstspierpoint.
Hopkins, Miss, Kermington, Ulceby.
Howell, A., Esq., Mayor, Welshpool, 2 copies.
Howell, Rev. G., Rectory, Llangattock, Crickhowell
Howell, Rev. D., St John's, Cardiff.
Howell, David, Esq., Solicitor, Machynlleth.
Hughes, H. R., Esq., Kinmel Park, Abergele, 4 copies.
Hughes, Rev. Dr., St John's Rectory, London, 4 copies.
Hughes, Rev. Joshua, Vicarage, Llandovery.
Hughes, Rev. Richard, Bodedern, Anglesey.
Hughes, Rev. J., Myrtle Hill, Llandeilo.
Hughes, Rev. J., Collierley, Gateshead-on-Tyne.
Hughes, J., Esq., Middleton, Manchester.
Hughes, W. Bulkeley, Esq., M.P., Plascoch, Anglesey, 3 copies.
Hughes, Rev. Alfred T., Vicarage, Aberavon.
Hughes, Rev. M., Vicar of Pentraeth, Anglesey.
Hughes, James, Esq., Manchester.
Hughes, Rev. W., Caerwys Rectory, Holywell.
Hughes, R. W., Esq., Bank, Beaumaris.
Hughes, Miss, Aberdare.
Hughes, Rev. David, Tredegar.
Hughes, Mr H., A.C.R.G., Anglesey.
Hughes, R. Jones, Esq., Plas-yn-llangoed, Beaumaris.
Hughes, Rev. R., Edge Hill, Liverpool.
Hughes, Miss, 7 West Bank Road, Liverpool.
Hughes & Son, Messrs, Wrexham.
Hughes, Thomas, Esq., Ystrad, Denbigh.
Hughes, Rev. H. P., Shuttleworth, Bury.

Humphreys, Thos., Esq., High Street, Manchester.
Hunt, John, Esq., Abercarn, Newport, Mon.

Ingman, A. B., Esq., High Street, Manchester.

James, Rev. Dr., Pantêg Rectory, Pontypool.
James, Rev. Jas., Llanbadarn Trefeglwys, Cardigan.
James, Rev. T., F.S.A., F.G.H.S. (Llallawg), Netherthong, Huddersfield.
James, Rev. D. Lloyd, Pontrobert Vicarage, Welshpool.
James, Rev. E., Rhys, Prestatyn, Rhyl.
James, Mr, Irewell House, Eccles.
James, Miss, Stoke Ferry, Brandon.
James, Rev. T., Marsh Gibbon, Bicester.
Jarret, Griffith, Esq., Glasfryn, Harrow-on-the-Hill, N.W.
Jenner, Mrs, Bryngarn, Bridgend, 2 copies.
Jenkins, Rev. R., B.A., Trefdraeth, Bangor.
Jenkins, Rev. John, Abbey Square, Chester.
Jenkins, John, Esq., Mayor, Ruthin.
Jenkins, Rev. W., Michaelstone-y-Vedw, Cardiff.
Jenkins, Peter R., Esq., Llangeitho, Lampeter.
Jenkins, Rev. J. D., St Fagan's, Aberdare.
Jones, Venerable Archdeacon, Liverpool.
Jones, Venerable Archdeacon Wynne, Anglesey.
Jones, Venerable Archdeacon W. Basil Tickel, York.
Jones, Rev. J., (Idrysin), Llandysilio, New Quay.
Jones, Rev. J. M., Incumbent of Rhos, Ruabon.
Jones, Rev. J., Rectory, Kilypebyll, Swansea.
Jones, Rev. T., Rector of Llanengan, Pwllheli.

Jones, Rev. T., Pentraeth, Anglesey.
Jones, Rev. Evan, Bodedern, Anglesey.
Jones, Rev. Charles, B.D., Chaplain to Lunatic Asylum, Bridgend.
Jones, Rev. Lewis, Almondbury, Huddersfield.
Jones, Rev. J. D. Colwyn, Conway.
Jones, Mr William, Glantraeth, Anglesey.
Jones, Hugh, Esq., Bodfeirig, Anglesey.
Jones, Richard, Esq. (Derfel), Spring Gardens, Manchester.
Jones, Rev. Ed., P.C., Bistre, Mold.
Jones, Rev. D., Brynffordd, Holywell.
Jones, Rev. D., Curate of Upper Bangor.
Jones, Mr Morgan, Manchester.
Jones, Rev. D., Ynysmudw, Swansea.
Jones, W., Esq., Pendre House, Mold.
Jones, Thomas, Esq., Manchester.
Jones, Rev. J., Curate, Brecon.
Jones, John, Esq., Westminster Buildings, Chester.
Jones, Rev. H. H., M.A., Llanidan, Anglesey.
Jones, Rev. R. Harris, Vicarage, Llanidloes.
Jones, Rev. Goodman, Rectory, Llangristiolus, Anglesey.
Jones, Robert, Esq., Bridge Street, Chester.
Jones, Mr Evan, Eastgate, Chester.
Jones, Mr J., National School, Gravesend.
Jones, Maurice, Esq., 7 St James Sq., Manchester.
Jones, John, Esq., 78 Richmond St., Manchester.
Jones, Robert, Esq., Clapham Common, London, 2 copies.
Jones, Sir Willoughby, Cranmer Hall, Fakenham.

Jones, Edward, Esq., Camden Street, Birmingham.
Jones, Rev. J., Vicarage, Llanarmon-yn-yale, Mold.
Jones, Rev. R., Llanarmon-yn-yale, Mold.
Jones, Hugh, Esq., Solicitor, Carnarvon.
Jones, J. Williams, Esq., Mold, 2 copies.
Jones, Messrs & Sons, Publishers, Aberdare.
Jones, Mr J., Nanty Plas, Llanbadrig.
Jones, Ellis, Esq., 6 Park View, Manchester.
Jones, W. O., Esq., Bowden, Manchester.
Jones, Miss, Ty'nllwyn, Corwen.
Jones, Rev. L. Price, Aberyscir, Brecon.
Jones, Rev. J. D., Blaengwenin, Llannon, Aberayron.
Jones, Rev. Thomas, Llandysul, Carmarthen.
Jones, Rev. John, Ystradmeurig, Tregaron.
Jones, Rev. John, Brynmawr, Newport, Mon.
Jones, Rev. J., Curate, Aberystwyth.
Jones, Rev. W. Jones, High Street, Tredegar.
Jones, Rev. John, Vicar of Abergwesin, Builth.
Jones, Rev. J. Powell, Vicarage, Llantrissant, Pontypridd.
Jones, Rev. J., Vicar of Llanfihangel-gene'r glyn, Aberystwyth.
Jones, Thomas, Esq., President of the Cheetham Library, Manchester, 2 copies.
Jones, William, Esq., Llwynygroes, Lampeter.
Jones, Rev. Joseph, Garmoyle Street, Belfast.
Jones, Thomas, Esq., Park Lane, Denbigh.
Jones, Rev. J. R., Kilsby, Glenview-Llanwrtyd, Builth.
Jones, Edward, Esq., Pendre House, Holywell.
Joseph, Joseph, Esq., Bank, Brecon, 2 copies.

Kay, Mrs, Crumpton Castle, Cheetham Hill, Manchester.
Kelly, T. T., Esq., Solicitor, Mold.

Lang, Rev. Ernest A., Rector of St Mary's, Manchester.
Laugharne, Rev. T., Llanbeulan, Anglesey.
Law, Mrs, Oxton, Birkenhead.
Lewis, Griffith, Esq., Alltacham, Pontardawe, Swansea.
Lewis, Rev. J., Llansadwrn, Anglesey.
Lewis, Rev. J. Haddon, Hunt.
Lewis, David, Esq., Picadilly, Manchester.
Lewis, Rev. L. Woodward, Vicar of Leysdown, Kent.
Lewis, John, Esq., Glynisa, Llangeitho, Lampeter.
Lewis, William, Esq., Snell St., Everton, Liverpool.
Lewis, Rev. E., Vicarage, Dolgelley.
Lewis, L., Esq., Nelson Emporium, Carnarvon.
Longcroft, C. R., Esq., Llanina, Aberayron, 2 copies.
Lloyd, Charles Spencer, Esq., Leaton Knolls, Shrewsbury, 3 copies.
Lloyd, Sir T. D., M.P., Bronwydd, Cardigan, 4 copies.
Lloyd, T. W., Esq., 112 Market Street, Manchester.
Lloyd, Rev. M., Llanylltyd, Dolgelley.
Lloyd, John, Esq., Bryngwran, Brynygors.
Lloyd, Bennett, Esq., 157 Snell Street, Everton, Liverpool.
Lloyd, Rev. Yarburgh Gamaliel, Sewerby House, Bridlington, 2 copies.
Lloyd, J., Esq., The Brow, Ruabon, 2 copies.
Lloyd, Rev. D., Trefonen Rectory, Oswestry.

Lloyd, Mr John, Glascow House, Mold.
Lloyd, Rev. T. R., Strata Florida, Tregaron.
Luxmore, Miss, Bryn-Asaph, St Asaph, 2 copies.

M'Alister, Mr, 14 Great George Street, Liverpool.
Mackenzie, W., Esq., Glasgow, 3 copies.
M'Neile, Rev. Dr, Toxteth Park, Liverpool.
Manley, Miss E., Hatchford Parsonage, Cobham.
Meredith, Rev. T., Newborough, Anglesey.
Meredith, Joseph, Esq., Hagley Road, Birmingham.
Michaelis, W., Esq., 10 Fountain St., Manchester.
Middleton, Rev. J. E., St Bees College.
Minshull, Mrs, Abergwynant, Beddgelert, 4 copies.
Morgan, Rev. D., Rector of Llanbadarnfawr, Radnor, 6 copies.
Morgan, G. Osborne, Esq., Lincoln's Inn, 2 copies.
Morgan, Rev. J., Glanogwen, Bangor.
Morgan, Rev. J. W., Beaufort, Newport, Mon.
Morgan, Rev. M. Price (Melancton) Vicarage, Llansamlet, Swansea.
Morgan, Rev. E., Syston, Leicester.
Morgan, Rev. H., Rhyl.
Morgan, J. W., Esq., Bolgoed, Brecon, 2 copies.
Morgan, Thomas, Esq., Manchester.
Morgan, Mr James, National School, Llanwrin, Machynlleth.
Morice, Rev. Thomas R. (Fellow of Jesus College, Oxford), Aberystwyth.
Morris, Rev. J., Llanallgo, Moelfra, Anglesey.
Morris, J. G., Esq., The Abbey, Grassandale, Liverpool, 2 copies.

SUBSCRIBERS' NAMES.

Nathan, Rev. J. F., Brynmawr, Newport, Mon.
Nichol, John, Esq., Merthyr Mawr, Bridgend, 2 copies.
Nixon, T. Jones, Esq., Birkenhead.

Oldfield, Benjamin, Esq., White Bear Inn, Manchester.
Openshaw, J., Esq., High Street, Manchester.
Overton, Wm., Esq., ex-Mayor, Wrexham, 2.copies.
Owen, Richard, Esq., 22 Bridge Street, Carnarvon, 2 copies.
Owen, T., Esq., Trefeilir, Anglesey.
Owen, Rev. Dr, Rectory, Trefdraeth, Anglesey.
Owen, Rev. H. D., Llangadwaldr, Anglesey.
Owen, Rev. D., Eglwysfach, Conway.
Owen, Rev. J., Christ Church, St Albans.
Owen, T. L., Esq., Regent House, Carnarvon.
Owen, Rev. H., Llanerchmedd.
Owen, Rev. J., Erryrys, Mold.
Owen, Mr Robert, Slate Merchant, Llandudno.
Owen, Mr Edward, Bryngoleu, Llanfairmathafarnathaf, Anglesey.
Owen, Owen, Esq., Solicitor, Pwllheli.
Owen Edward, Esq., Upper Northgate St., Chester.
Owen, Rev. Owen, Tredegar, Newport, Mon.
Owen, R. Baugh, Esq., Turf Square, Carnarvon.
Owen, Mr George, Tea Merchant, Carnarvon.

Palmer, Sir Roundel, 6 Portland Place, London, W., 2 copies.
Parry, Rev. D. (Dewi Mochryn), Tredegar.
Parry, T. T., Esq., Bod-difyr, Bangor.

Parry, Cain, Esq., Mold, 2 copies.
Parry, John, Esq., Mercer, Bangor.
Parry, Rev. Henry, Llanllechyd, Bangor.
Peel, Edmund, Esq., Brynypys, Rhuabon, 4 copies.
Philips, Captain, Rhual, Mold, 4 copies.
Philips, Sir Thomas, Temple, London, 2 copies.
Philips, Rev. E., Aberanell, near Builth.
Philips, Rev. E. Owen, M.A., Vicarage, Aberystwyth.
Philips, Rev. John, Fron, Bangor, 2 copies.
Pierce, Hugh, Esq., 47 Sefton Square, Liverpool, 2 copies.
Pierce & Thompson, Messrs, 57 Caryl St., Liverpool.
Pickmore, John Richard, Vyrniew Mount, Llanfair, Welshpool.
Poole, Rev. J. W., Rector of Aberfraw, Anglesey.
Powell, Mr Thomas, 13 Dean Street, Aberdare.
Powell, Evan, Esq., St Mary's Villa, Newtown, Montgomery.
Preswell, Miss M. Jardine, Totness.
Price, Owen, Esq., Cafna, Llanfechell.
Price, Mrs, Rhiwlas, Bala.
Price, William, Esq., Solicitor, Glan-nant-y-llan Llanffoist, Abergavenny.
Price, Rev. H. F., College, Cheltenham.
Price, Rev. Dr, Box Cottage, Aberdare, 2 copies.
Prichard, Rev. Rees, Vicarage, Llandyfodwg, Bridgend.
Pring, William, Esq., Mold.
Pring & Price, Messrs, Mold.
Pryce, Rev. James, St Thomas, Groeston, Carnarvon.

Proctor & Ryland, Messrs, Saltney, Chester, 2 copies.
Pugh, Mr D. G., Registry Office, St Asaph.
Pughe, Rev. E., Rectory, Llantrisant, Holyhead.
Pughe, J., Esq., F.R.C.S.J.P., Brynawel, Aberdovey.

Randles, J., Esq., 10 Meal Street, Manchester.
Reece, W. H., Esq., Oakfield Cottage, Edgebaston, Birmingham.
Rees, Mr Edward, Medical Hall, Machynlleth.
Rees, Rev. Thomas, Vicarage, Llanishen, Cardiff.
Rees, R. O., Esq., Chemist, &c., Dolgelly, 2 copies.
Rees, Rev. W., D.D., 80 Elizabeth St., Liverpool.
Remison, R. C., Esq., Alma Place, Headingly, Leeds.
Reynolds, Dr, Friars, St Michael's Hamlet, Liverpool, 2 copies.
Richards, C., Esq., Bank Buildings, Llangollen.
Richards, Rev. H., St Fagans, Aberdare.
Richards, Rev. R., Horwich, Bolton, Lancashire, 3 copies.
Richards, Mr D., Penydarren, Myrthyr-Tydvil.
Richards, Mr Morgan, High Bailiff, County Court, Bangor.
Roberts, R., Esq., Royal Bank Buildings, Liverpool, 2 copies.
Roberts, Dr, Mosley Street, Manchester, 2 copies.
Roberts, T. F., Esq., Portland Street, Manchester.
Roberts, Mr Griffith, Coventry House, Carnarvon.
Roberts, Rev. D., Coity, Bridgend.
Roberts, John, Esq., Glandwr, Carnarvon.

Roberts, John, Esq., Garston, Liverpool.
Roberts, David, Esq., 65 Hope Street, Liverpool.
Roberts, Edward, Esq., Liverpool.
Roberts, J. E., Esq., 104 Mill Street, Liverpool.
Roberts, R., Esq., Bodran, London House, High Street, Rhyl.
Roberts, Mr John, Relieving Officer, Mold.
Roberts, R., Esq., Registry Office, St Asaph.
Robert, T., Esq., 15 Mount Street, Alton Hotel, Manchester.
Roberts, William, Esq., Firgrove, Lydiate, Ormskirk, 2 copies.
Roper, G. T. E., Esq., Solicitor, Mold.
Rowlands, Rev. J., Incumbent of Pwllycibau, Llanfyllin.
Rowlands, H., Esq., 10 Meal Street, Manchester.
Rowlands, Rev. Daniel, Llanidloes.
Rowbotham, A., Esq., Alexandra Buildings, Liverpool.

Sadler, Wm., Esq., 22 Fountain St., Manchester.
Salisbury, E. R. G., Esq., Glan-Aber, Chester, 2 copies.
Salisbury, T., Esq., Jackson Street, Tonge, Middleton, Manchester.
Salisbury, Rev. E. E., Baylee, B.D., Thundersley Rectory, Raleigh, Essex.
Salisbury, Hon. and Rev. L. S., Llanwern, Newport, Mon, 2 copies.
Sandbach, H. R., Esq., Hafodunos, Llanwrst, 2 copies.
Sandwith, Dr B. C., Llanrhaidr Hall, Denbigh.

SUBSCRIBERS' NAMES.

Schabe, Mrs, Rhodes House, Manchester, 2 copies.
Salter, Jackson, Esq., Mayor, Oswestry, 2 copies.
Shaw, J. G., Esq., The Cross, Chester.
Sisson, R. J., Esq., Talardy, St Asaph.
Smallpiece, Rev. T., M.A., St Bees College.
Smith, Mrs, Stanley House, Eccleshall, 4 copies.
Smith, Martin, Esq., Parklane, Denbigh.
Smith, Mr James, Trefdraeth, Bangor.

Thirlwall, Rev. T. J., Rectory, Nantmel, Rhyader.
Thomas, Rev. W. B., Steynton, Milford Haven.
Thomas, Rev. D., H. M. Inspector of Schools, Anglesey.
Thomas, Rev. W., M.A., Llwynrhydowen, Llandysul.
Thomas, Rev. D. W., St Ann's, Bangor.
Thomas, Rev. C. D., Bettws, Llanrwst.
Thomas, Rev. D. R., Rectory, Cefn, St Asaph.
Thomas, Rev. D., Rector of Margam, Bridgend.
Thomas, Mr Thomas, 8 Dean Street, Aberdare.
Thomas, Rev. Thomas, Rector of Disserth, Builth.
Thomas, Rev. Thomas, Pontypool.
Thomas, John, Esq., Architect and County Surveyor, Carnarvon.
Thomas, Rev. T., Tredegar.
Thomas, W. R., Esq., (Jesus College, Oxford), Tregaron.
Thornycroft, Rev. J., Thornycroft, Congleton, 2 copies.
Tomlinson, E., Esq., Eccles, Manchester.
Tracey, The Hon. C. M., M.P., 2 copies.
Traherne, Mrs, St Hilary, Cowbridge, 2 copies.

Turner, Llewellyn, Esq., Mayor, Carnarvon.
Twentyman, Rev. J., Edge Hill, Liverpool.
Tynte, Col. Kemeys, M.P., Cefn Mably, 2 copies.

Walker, W., Esq., Bank, Mold.
Walmsley, Gilbert G., Esq., 50 Lord St., Liverpool.
Whalley, J. Hammond, Esq., M.P., Plasmadoc, 3 copies.
White, Rev. Dr, Islington, Liverpool.
Williams, Sir Hugh, Bodelwydden, Rhyl, 4 copies.
Williams, Rev. J., Hope Vicarage, Mold, 2 copies.
Williams, Rev. Thomas, Rectory, St George, St Asaph.
Williams, Rev. D., Dilyfe, Machynlleth.
Williams, Rev. T., Brocklesby, Ulceby.
Williams, Ven. Archdeacon, Carmarthen.
Williams, H. O., Esq., Trecastell, Beaumaris.
Williams, Owen, Esq., 32 Castle Street, Liverpool.
Williams, Rev. Chancellor, Basaleg, Newport, Mon.
Williams, Mr Thomas, Brynmeilir, Anglesey.
Williams, W. Maysmor, Esq., ex-Mayor, Chester.
Williams, Rev. J., Eglwysfach, Conway.
Williams, Mr J. Prydderch (Rhydderch o Fôn), Rhyl.
Williams, Rev. D., Nannerch Vicarage, Mold.
Williams, Mr Benjamin, Fron, Mold.
Williams, Rev. J. H., Llangadwaldr, Anglesey.
Williams, Rev. Canon Wynne, Menaifron, Anglesey.
Williams, Mr Phillip, Bridge Street, Aberystwyth, 2 copies.
Williams, Rev. J. (Glanmor), Whitehaven.
Williams, Rev. Robt., Rectory, Llanfaclog, Anglesey.
Williams, John, Esq., Penyback, Kidwelly.

Williams, Rev. D., Rhydybont, Lampeter.
Williams, Richard, Esq., Treban, Bryngwran, Anglesey.
Williams, Rev. D., Penmaenmawr, Conway.
Williams, Rev. Thos., Grammar School, Cowbridge.
Williams, Joel, Esq., Mold.
Williams, Llewellyn, Esq., Felinheli, Holyhead.
Williams, Rev. W., Tyddyn, Pentraeth, 2 copies.
Williams, Watkin, Esq., Fig Tree Court, Temple, 4 copies.
Williams, Rev. L. E., Pontyberun, Llanelly.
Williams, W., Esq., Plasgwyn, Pentraeth, 2 copies.
Williams, J., Esq., Coal Merchant, Gloucester.
Williams, The Hon. Lady Sarah Hay, Rhianva, Bangor, 2 copies.
Williams, Dr, Mold.
Williams, Mr Thomas R., Sculptor, 48 Welcombe Street, Hulme.
Williams, Mr David, 1 George Street, George Town, Merthyr-Tydvil.
Williams, Robert, Esq., Ty-ucha, Mold.
Williams, Rev. D., St David's College, Lampeter.
Wilcox, Rev. H. Menevensis, Aberdare.
Winstone, Rev. W., Llwyncyntefin, Sunny Bridge, Brecon.
Wood, Mrs, Halling Grove, Penkridge, 4 copies.
Wright, Clifford, Esq., Mount Torrel, Loughborough.

www.ingramcontent.com/pod-product-compliance
Lightning Source LLC
Chambersburg PA
CBHW031937230426
43672CB00010B/1955